Permission to Observe:

Extraordinary Stories from an Ordinary Medical Career

By

Gregory R. Frost, RRT

Cover Image

Leper Hole St. Luke's Church - Duston, England.

Believed to have been used by lepers to observe Mass.

Photo courtesy of David Blackburn.

Cover design by Abigail V. Schmidt.

—Introduction—

Sometimes I do things in stages. I wrote the first lines of this book on December 23, 1995 then promptly forgot about it. Life gets busy. The project collected dust for the better part of two decades. I later stumbled upon it while searching for a copy of my resume in the hope of escaping a mundane job as a high school Library Assistant (at the time well into my fifties).

Although the library job was personally rewarding, it was financially disastrous. The discovery of my initial notes however, turned out to be one of the best things that could have happened, and the impetus for this book.

When I first got the notion to write a collection of stories involving life and death in the operating room as witnessed by an outsider (sales rep), I thought that would be enough... hence the title. The original idea for an opening story was to describe my first surgery as a suture sales rep while my prospective customer (the surgeon) evaluated the product.

The case that day involved a routine *open retropubic suspension* (more commonly known as a bladder tie-up). This is done to relieve stress incontinence for patients who suffer from chronic urine leaks, often at the slightest onset of laughter, cough, or sneeze.

The procedure was performed by a prominent urology surgeon in the Midwest. The doctor, known for his light-hearted approach to life and work was chatty that particular day and eager to try the samples.

With my hair scrunched inside an uncomfortable pancake-shaped cover, my mask tightly in place, and the rest of my body covered by an ill-fitting set of thin blue scrubs with the pockets missing... I felt exposed and vulnerable.

Half way through the operation, sweat trickled down both sides of my neck and I could barely think when the surgeon finally spoke. The urologist, along with his team of scrub nurses, instrument tech, and anesthesiologist, were quite relaxed—having a grand old time actually.

On the other hand, I agonized over the stress of it all. My feet were killing me from standing motionless for over an hour in new, stiff dress shoes that were covered by hot paper booties. Suddenly I thought *What if the guy was really a jerk and asked a question to purposely throw me off? What if I had to use the bathroom or sneeze or blow my nose?* All of which I did. *How come I was the only one in the room with scrubs that were too tight and sweat-drenched?*

What finally helped break the tension was when the surgeon, closing the wound with my suture and shifting his weight from one foot to the other casually voiced the question, "Has anybody ever tasted urine?" No response. "No I'm not kidding. When it comes out, you know, for the most part it's sterile." Still no response. "It's really not that bad," he insisted. One of the scrub nurses turned, slapping a pair of scissors in his hand and muffled through her mask, "You know you're crazy. Can't we just get this done? I go on break in ten minutes."

Laughter followed, and for the first time I was able to relax a bit. I had this mental picture of the doctor swirling yellow fluid in a long-stemmed glass—offering a stuffy commentary about the sample being 'fruity, yet cloudy, with hints of asparagus and musk'. From then on, I knew the stories would be unique, and the OR would be unlike any other workplace.

What occurred to me after locating the long lost paragraph was that I had enough material to begin the tale twenty years earlier...in 1974 - the year I graduated from Respiratory Therapy training. I was hired at a large St. Louis hospital and my first day on the job as an Inhalation

Therapist sets the stage for the book's opening story inside a very hot, dark, and busy Intensive Care Unit.

A few of the stories go beyond my Respiratory Therapy career, capturing some of the highlights (and lowlights) of four decades in healthcare, beginning in high school with the humblest of jobs—the Transport Orderly.

The duties of the Transport Orderly primarily involved delivering freshly obtained specimens to the respective labs for analysis. For example, containers of blood, urine, feces, tumors, sputum, and the like were picked up (and occasionally dropped) on a daily basis. But the role also required the repositioning of patients—from bed to stretcher and so on. And of course, the ultimate transport—those who unexpectedly required a last minute lift to the morgue.

All of the stories, either expressed first hand or shared by colleagues are based on actual events and observations. Every error, whether technical, clinical, or otherwise, is mine.

Names of individuals, organizations, locations, and certain details have been altered for obvious reasons.

—Acknowledgements—

The gaps in my knowledge are significant, which is why I am indebted to a few individuals in particular:

Dianne Koehnecke, PhD, my first college English professor who has been a great source of encouragement and support.

Retired Police Chief Robert J. Noonan who offered helpful details regarding the crime mentioned in chapter two.

Jan Ellersieck, an extraordinary history teacher who painstakingly reviewed the manuscript and provided the constructive criticism I need.

John Wienstroer, a talented perfectionist who provided exceptional editing.

Jaime Pillai who first suggested I come full circle and return to patient care.

Carol Frost, for proof reading the manuscript and believing in me.

Texas State University Professor and Pulitzer Prize finalist Tim O'Brien said it best. In his great work on the Vietnam experience, *The Things They Carried*, he sums up what purpose stories really serve—what they have done for him, and will continue to do for others:

"All you can do is tell it one more time, patiently, adding and subtracting, making up a few things to get at the truth."

"Bear with me a little, and I will show you"
The book of Job

—In Memory—
Ryan Matthew Frost
November 13, 1976 – April 27, 1983

Proceeds from this book will help support families of children with complex and catastrophic illnesses in the St. Louis area.

—Forward—

It was at the scrub sink, twenty years ago, that I met Greg Frost. When he asked about my last name, we realized that we had grown up in St. Louis only a few blocks from each other. My older brother and he were in the same class. When I left on a mission trip to Papua New Guinea, Greg didn't forget me, and sent medical supplies (including respiratory equipment and Davis & Geck suture) which were greatly needed and appreciated.

Everyone in the medical field shares a common bond. It is a bond that comes from a life of service to one's patients, and it is a bond that is strengthened by stories. In this book, Frost has drawn on his own lifetime of service to assemble this extraordinary collection of humorous, thought-provoking, and ultimately, inspirational stories.

As Will Rogers said "People's minds are changed through observation and not through argument." I firmly believe that people who share the bond of medicine will connect with the stories told here, and after the stories are over, they will return to their patients with renewed enthusiasm and joy.

Roy J. Elfrink M.D., FACS

Desire

—Chapter 1—

Debut

"The first essential is to have your nerves
well in hand."

William Osler, M.D.
Valedictory Address, University of Pennsylvania
May 1, 1889

PERMISSION TO OBSERVE

It wasn't the ribbon of blood trickling from the incision and wandering down the side of her throat that bothered me. Neither did the way her jaw thrust upward at such an awful angle because of the eight-pound sandbag wedged beneath her shoulder blades.

With her chin aimed at the stained yellow ceiling tiles of the St. Bartholomew ICU, she seemed to be pointing the way to heaven. Her neck and forehead had begun to sweat under the blinding spotlight that was targeted dead center on her gullet, exposing all that is precious and vulnerable in her dark, thick neck.

But she was oblivious.

Above the deep, sweaty crease circling her lower neck, the doctor made a second, deeper incision through the rings of the trachea, and thrust the first two knuckles of his gloved index finger through the opening. Her reflex cough was a desperate but futile effort to cough-out the digital attack. When the surgeon did withdraw his finger, a sizeable mucus plug exploded out of the hole and landed at the foot of the bed.

Of course, she didn't realize that her throat had just been slit. She didn't realize anything. Hattie Mae Johnson was in a deep coma, and perilously close to death.

It was my first day on the job as a Respiratory Therapy technician at the old St. Bartholomew Hospital in St. Louis and already my job was stressful. I was hired as a night-shift technician, partly because I was in the process of completing my training at Maryville College. The other reason was that they needed a warm body on nights.

My excitement at the prospect of donning the coveted white coat and strolling down the hall was reward enough. When I finally did get the chance to wear what felt like Joseph's coat of many colors, I was sure my stethoscope would be carefully coiled in my left pocket, better yet, draped around my shoulders, as if I'd just finished examining a patient in a life or death crisis.

I looked as good as any first year resident. Unfortunately, St. Bart's was not a teaching hospital. No residents, medical students, or interns ever showed up, so I quickly became a legend in my own mind.

Yet to finally be recognized as a healthcare team member, and be paid to experience life and death drama created an enthusiasm that amazed (but mostly annoyed) my department co-workers.

"You'll get over it Frost," was the most common response to my eagerness to volunteer for just about any department task. They would offer such remarks (almost in unison) as they plopped down on a badly worn, green faux leather sofa, lighting up cigarettes to silence their own coughs.

Rumbling loose any left-over phlegm built up since the last smoke break—they would clear their throats and proceed upstairs to perform the next set of IPPB treatments (intermittent positive pressure breathing) and check the patients on ventilators.

After the obligatory meeting in the Personnel department that first morning wrapping up all the tedious paperwork, our department director, Richard Lessman, issued my marching orders for the day. I was to shadow the other technicians and therapists to observe as much as possible, noting their approach to patients and how to best interact with the medical staff and administration (the nuns). We were to display the highest level of professional decorum at all times. The Sisters expected no less.

* * *

I learned during orientation that the hospital was actually one of the oldest Catholic institutions in the country and maintained a long tradition of care provided by the Sisters of St. Bartholomew. The nun-managed philosophy permeated the organization; patients first, doctors second, nurses third, and staff (of my caliber)... somewhere near the bottom of the St. Bart food chain.

The 225-bed, mission-based facility seemed sorely out of place in the middle of an old city residential section. Sandwiched between dozens of look-alike brick two-story flats, the hospital loomed above what was (and remains today) one of the roughest parts of the city. What better place to begin a career?

*   *   *

Things were actually going smoothly the first day. I was sailing along from one room to the next, joking with patients and nurses, surprisingly comfortable in my new role with little to no responsibility—until I heard my name blaring on the hospital's crackly, overhead speaker system like the trumpet before a battle.

I had just returned to the department for some oxygen supplies to replenish a crash cart on one of the floors. The blasts came through at a decibel level equivalent to that of an F-15 at takeoff. *Greg Frost... call extension 4-1-5; Greg Frost... 4-1-5.* I had never before heard my name bellowed like that from a loud speaker.

"That for me?" I asked as I shot a look at Verla, the only other person in the department, who had come back for a smoke. She looked my way as she lit up, crooked one eye brow and turned to pick up an old National Enquirer. Short of a cardiac arrest, nothing was going to interrupt her break as she eased into the sofa.

When I picked up the phone and dialed the extension, Phyllis, our day shift supervisor, answered from one of the nursing stations. She told me that I should report directly to the fourth floor ICU. I heard her take a deep drag on her cigarette and said, "Better make it STAT." I started to tell her I'd meet her there, but she had already hung up.

Whatever it was carried a genuine sense of urgency. My job was to go—and go I did. I hung up the phone and rushed out the two heavy, metal office doors, pulling wisps of smoke along with me. As the adrenalin surged, my heart pounded and my hands shook. Thoughts raced as I opted for the stairs over the elevator to save a few seconds.

What in the world was going on in the ICU, and how could they *possibly* think I could contribute anything on my first day? And if it was a code (cardiac arrest), why wasn't it being announced as one? What were they thinking? I hadn't even found the bathrooms yet!

Hopping two steps at a time, I passed three nurses in the stairwell on their way to the cafeteria for a coffee break. In that brief contact, I'm sure I detected at least one snicker. They all seemed to know where I was headed and for some reason found it amusing. It didn't take long for me to figure out that every one of my co-workers was either tied up with a patient, taking a smoke somewhere, or simply out of pager range. That left *me* to cover whatever was already underway in the ICU.

I had no idea what I was walking into. I had heard some details in morning report about Hattie Mae *still* alive and on a vent; that she had a dangerously low blood oxygen level; that the mucus suctioned from her airway tube was noted as 'thick, yellow, and tenacious'; and that she was expected to code—unless a surgical procedure was performed.

The procedure (tracheotomy) involved creating a new airway opening in the neck, and would eliminate the breathing tube anchored in her throat connecting her to the ventilator. I had learned in school that patients who were ventilator-dependent for extended periods began to develop serious complications.

Along with severe trauma to the airways from the constant friction of the endotracheal (ET) tube rubbing against the tissues; the delicate balance of blood chemistry often became lop-sided, resulting in the patient 'crashing'.

Hattie Mae was crashing.

One thing my instructors neglected to touch on in school, however, was the fact that when you summon a large group of individuals who are scattered throughout a thirty year-old hospital building, to suddenly swarm into a single, poorly ventilated ICU room on a humid July morning in St. Louis—the unpredictable becomes inevitable.

* * *

Dr. Jerome Cleveland, longtime staff physician and the designated surgeon on-call, was paged early that morning and asked to perform the tracheotomy on Hattie Mae. Dr. Cleveland, beady-eyed in his Harry Carey-style square glasses and thick handlebar mustache bore an uncanny resemblance to the lead singer of the 70's pop group, The Spinners. I wanted to ask him if he had a twin brother somewhere in Motown. Whenever we passed each other in the halls or out on the parking lot that stupid *"Rubber Band Man"* tune got stuck in my head. I envisioned him stopping dead in his tracks, opening his medical bag, and pulling out a huge, elastic band to dance through his rounds. For the longest time, I had trouble separating that image from reality.

Along with the doctor, representatives from several departments making up the cardiac arrest team were paged simultaneously and had quickly assembled in the ICU for the procedure. The team included a lab technician (to draw blood), x-ray and EKG technicians, a pharmacist to help dispense fluids, an anesthetist to intubate the patient, a respiratory therapist to manage the airway, at least one nurse and nursing supervisor. The unofficial team, however, often included a security guard, a unit secretary, possibly an orderly or two, someone from housekeeping, the maintenance guy (if one happened to wander by), and of course, the 'POD' (priest on duty). Add to the group, one very large, very sick bed-ridden patient tethered to three monitors, an assortment of intravenous bags, a washing machine-size mechanical ventilator—compress all of that into a small, pitifully air-conditioned hospital room and you have the makings of hell in a box.

When I reached the ICU and made my way into the room, I realized what was happening. I couldn't take my eyes off Hattie's neck which was about to be flayed open. Maybe it was the light that got to me, or the position of her head as her forehead was being pressed down by a pair of hands coming from somewhere behind the headboard, pushing it deep into the pillow so the surgeon would have as wide a field of vision as possible.

The dingy, flexible lamp used as an overhead bore scars of its own and added more heat to the room than light. Dented and scratched, the lamp was aimed directly on Hattie's neck, like a hunter's flashlight on the eyes of its prey. Except this prey was already at the mercy of the hunter.

A red, two-inch-long cleft was created when Dr. Cleveland made his incision. The 'lips' of the wound were quickly stretched wide by two Jackson retractor clips, forming a diamond-shape wound that revealed sparkling reddish-pink flesh sliding in one direction while the dark brown skin covering it moved in the opposite direction, all shifting with the rhythm of the ventilator.

My senses were raped.

The heat, the people, the sweat, the noise, the yellow ceiling, the green-spotted linoleum floor... all the white coats... *My lab coat! What if some kind of unidentified muck got on my new lab coat? It's the only one I have! Would I ever be able to get the stain out? What if a flying mucus plug landed on my sleeve? I'd have to work one-armed for the rest of the day!*

But everything I saw, heard, and felt couldn't compare with what I soon realized was making me feel so awful. What hit me the hardest wasn't the blood, or the chaotic sounds, or the heat itself—it was the pervading *odor.* That raw, meaty, old deli-case smell—sweetly familiar, yet out of place here.

The combination of rubbing alcohol and musk, mixed with the humidity and body heat from the dozen or so employees jammed together, coupled with the stagnant air of the ICU created a bouquet like no other.

As I squeezed my way through the crowd, trying to follow my directive—to maintain professional demeanor—a more distinct and familiar aroma began wafting into my nostrils. At first, I thought someone farted. *Really? In this tiny meat locker?* Then I realized it wasn't a fart—it was feces. When Dr.Cleveland's finger slid into Hattie Mae's newly opened trachea, temporarily plugging it, she responded by producing an explosive cough and promptly messed herself... and it was a mess.

At that moment I was thankful for having made the choice *not* to pursue a career in nursing, where I could very well have been deemed the linen-changer following this affair. Surviving on I.V. fluid alone, intestines would normally be expected to produce little waste material, if any. In Hattie Mae's case, there must have been remnants of something. It was extraordinarily foul and I was embarrassed for her.

The others in the room, however, were unfazed. Then, one of the nurses turned up the oxygen flow coming from the wall, creating a whiff of pungent vinyl that filled the air. Packages of instruments and other items were torn open and placed on the bed adding to the sharp, plastic, new car-like smell.

8

I became disoriented. The odors blending in my nose didn't really fit with where I was. It was like standing in an automobile show room, enjoying that scent you associate with the anticipation and excitement of buying a new car— and then someone's infant suddenly fills a diaper… ruining the experience and transforming something pleasant into something disgusting.

Layer upon layer of perspiration soaked my clothes. I just knew that the freshly-pressed coat I was so proud of now sported a wide damp streak between my shoulders. In my battle with anxiety, the sweat was winning the war and I wanted to retreat. I can now testify to the fact that under extremely stressful conditions like this, it is possible to feel every pore of your skin empty like a bucket being poured.

I looked around the room and noticed the faces of the team members. They weren't paying particular attention to what was going on under the light. I thought every eye would be riveted on the scene playing out before us. The raw, naked underworld of glistening tissues, gliding textures and those gloved hands—exploring and manipulating things just so.

But I was the only one mesmerized. The others were, for the most part, engaged in little social pockets of discussion—all while Hattie Mae's life hung precariously in the balance. *"What'd you watch on TV last night?"* I heard from one corner. From another, *"Hey, have you seen that new Deliverance movie yet? Man, I couldn't believe that part in the woods when the guy squealed like a pig!"*

My dread worsened when the doctor prepared to make his *second* cut, the one beneath the skin—in the trachea itself, when he unexpectedly looked around and asked, "Anybody goin' to the Q-King today? I sure could use some barbecue."

Barbecue? Was that it? *That's* what I signed up for? Smack in the middle of a theater of life and death and you're worried about *lunch*? Incredible. Yet, over the years, I have grown to appreciate comments like that. The mounting tension in a crisis is sometimes unbearable, and when a flippant comment is made at the right time, it can provide great relief and a chance to take a step back and refocus.

Dr. Cleveland ordered the nurses to spread the two Jackson retractors—which looked like shiny escargot forks—just a little bit more, making the bloody opening wider still. He then positioned the edge of the scalpel blade and pushed straight down, popping it through the center of Hattie's tiny, ribbed trachea.

More blood... more mucus... more sweat... machine alarms.

And that hot, sweet smell.

Satisfied with the stab wound, he positioned the white plastic Shiley tracheotomy tube in his left hand, inserting and rotating the device through the opening so as to follow the natural contour of Hattie Mae's airway. The action produced a sound much like that of a hot air balloon valve opening.

Just as he slid the tube into place and reconnected her to the ventilator, the machine cycled with a deep inspiration. A loud rush of air was heard, interrupting the on-going dialog about how *Deliverance* had *really* ended; about how in the world they had made it down that waterfall alive; about whether or not the hillbilly Jon Voight had managed to impale was the right guy after all; and all that chewed-up flesh dangling from the leg of Burt Reynolds.

"Boy didn't that leg gash look real?" I heard. But I thought, *this* is what's real—here in the ICU isn't it? And if it is, why isn't everyone paying attention and concentrating on it like me instead of debating movies? Having watched so many trachs cut they were sure they knew how it would end.

But they would be wrong.

*   *   *

Dr. Cleveland seemed to sense something was amiss. He began looking around the room, deliberately making eye contact with several people before adjusting the tube's cuff pressure. This would seal off the trachea and allow the tube to become the body's new air pathway. As I watched the small pilot bulb being inflated and deflated over and over with an air-filled syringe, I realized that the three-inch curved tube of plastic I'd just seen in Dr. Cleveland's hand was now buried deep in Hattie's throat.

I suddenly felt the surging temperature in the room again and the growing wet spot on my back. The stench from feces lingered in the back of my throat and I heard the eardrum-bursting buzzes coming from the ventilator alarms as Hattie Mae tried her hardest to spew out the tube with each breath and cough.

I no longer heard the *Deliverance* conversation, nor could I see Dr. Cleveland's eyes, which, I was later told, had just come to rest on me.

Instead, what I saw was the scuffed, green linoleum floor filling my field of vision. Blurry, to be sure... but it was there. I thought for a second I was actually close enough to feel gritty bumps of paint on my cheek from the printed pattern of the floor tiles. Yes, I was sure that was the floor I was feeling—and tasting.

But just as quickly, it began to move.

The tiles were being pulled away from me, like the view of earth from a side-mounted NASA camera just launched. And what began as a narrow streak of perspiration on the center of my back had quickly spread into a full-body drench. My head throbbed, my legs shook, I was nauseated and everything was a blur. I felt several hands pulling and lifting me by my armpits. That's when I realized that this heroic, young code-4 team member had just fainted.

*   *   *

The two ICU nurses who'd come to my aid helped me over to the only place I could sit down—the visitor's chair at the foot of Hattie Mae's bed (which is exactly what I felt like—a visitor). Disoriented and soaked with perspiration, I could barely lift my head to make out the unmistakable scowl on Dr. Cleveland's face. If that wasn't enough, one of the nurses leaned over and asked if I'd had any blood work done lately, that maybe I should pay my doctor a visit to see exactly what was *wrong* with me.

And I thought I was ready for this stuff!

As I sat in the chair trying to look inconspicuous while desperately hoping to regain some dignity, it occurred to me that maybe the reason I couldn't see very well was the fact my eyes apparently had rolled back in the process of fainting and I had lost my contacts.

Great.

"I have to find my contacts," I said, loud enough for the room to hear. For an instant, I thought Hattie Mae was going to sit up, cock her head and start railing at me—shaking a finger in my direction for interrupting her procedure and acting like a fool. Of course, she didn't.

The same two nurses joined me in my search by dropping to all fours next to the bed, and began sliding their palms in wide circles on the floor. Scooting around and weaving through white nylon-covered legs and flapping lab coats, with our butts high in the air we looked like a lost train of Muslims in prayer. I could feel at least twelve sets of eyes burning into the back of my already wet coat, much like the spotlight aimed at Hattie's neck. This was *not* the kind of fame I needed.

* * *

Despite the chaos surrounding Hattie Mae's bed, Dr. Cleveland managed to ignore us and complete his task. He secured the tube by tying a soft white strip of cotton material around the back of Hattie's neck and then slid a thin sterile suction catheter through the newly created airway, burying it to the hilt. He placed one finger over the catheter's vent hole to create a vacuum while slowly pulling and rotating out the cloudy 18-inch tube.

Thick globs of yellow-green mucus did a slow-motion roll up the core of the tube and blasted their way through the top of the collection canister like a mighty garden hose belch.

With her mouth free of the endotracheal tube and her neck wound freshly dressed, Hattie Mae looked like new.

Except we all knew she wasn't.

Hattie Mae Johnson didn't have a chance. She just couldn't be weaned from the ventilator after her procedure and eventually died of complications from a staph infection combined with congestive heart failure and pneumonia.

*   *   *

In the months that followed, I wondered if my intrusion that day was part of the reason everything went south for her. Maybe it's not being completely fair to suggest that the distraction I caused was significant enough to throw Dr. Cleveland off. Having cut countless tracheotomies in his career, his skill was unmatched and he did exactly what needed to be done. At the same time, though, he *must* have been entertaining thoughts of lunch before ever walking into the room.

Maybe that's the mark of a confident surgeon and consummate professional, one who refuses to carry the weight of the world on his shoulders and can readily adapt to the crisis at hand.

*   *   *

We never did find my contacts. I remember a nurse asking during my crawl-search as drops of sweat rinsed the lime green linoleum, if I had ever thought to check *my eyes*. She said that contacts can sometimes drift off center, and you may not even realize they're really there.

She was right. When I stepped into Hattie Mae's tiny bathroom, pulled down my lower lids and peered in the smudged mirror, sure enough, there they were. Two glorious little green plastic bubbles, worth at least three paychecks.

Sliding them up and back into position, I quickly thanked the nurses and apologized for my lack-luster debut. I made a weak attempt to acknowledge the surgeon by nodding at him as he snapped off his gloves and turned to meet with the family.

He ignored me, so I quickly exited the room, anxious to distance myself from the whole ugly experience and everyone involved.

On his way to the waiting room, Dr. Cleveland noticed me standing outside the ICU entrance. As he walked through the door he stopped, squared to face me, and looked me straight in the eye. I braced, praying that I wouldn't hear something that would forever scar me and destroy my entire (one-day) career.

Instead, he offered some sage advice and encouraging wisdom gained from decades of experience.

"Next time," he instructed, "Get the baby backs. They're the best."

He smiled and walked away.

—Chapter 2—

A Death in the Family

"Self-preservation is the first law of nature;
Self-sacrifice is the highest rule of grace"

Luc de Clapiers, marquis de Vauvenargue,
18th century French author

Permission to Observe

In 1839, cholera came to visit. It was a disaster of mighty proportions. More than five thousand were lost to the epidemic. Worse, the region had no healthcare system in place. This set the stage for the nuns of St. Bartholomew—a small group of Sisters who funded their operation with faith instead of cash. Traveling to St. Louis by train on a heroic mission of mercy, the Sisters were among the first to begin any kind of organized approach to healthcare. Remarkably, the nuns were able to scrimp enough money to purchase a small city building shortly after arriving which served as their living quarters as well as the main treatment center.

One of the more unusual stories to come out of St. Bartholomew's beginning involved the location of the operating room. As the patient load steadily grew, the need to perform surgeries increased. Since cash was virtually non-existent, the designated surgery table was a long heavy wooden structure resembling a picnic bench you might see today in any park. All of the surgeries were performed on the table in the morning, and at day's end, the surface was wiped down, the area tidied-up, and the women would then be able to use the table to enjoy their evening meal. Not surprisingly, a large percentage of post-op complications involved the removal of splinters, which caused serious infections on the back-side of patients.

Sir Joseph Lister, considered the father of modern surgical practice and an active proponent of what would later become sterile technique, would only have been a youngster of twelve at the time. The world of medicine would have to wait.

When I worked at St. Bart's in the early 1970's, the power of the managing nuns was legendary. Many of the Sisters were stoic, devoid of humor and demanded respect at all times. Although not Catholic, I was practically expected to genuflect as we crossed paths in those dimly lit halls—the

Sisters forever adorned in their "Flying Nun" caps that were sharp as cactus spines. With calf-length habits swishing to and fro as they patrolled the halls, they mimicked a marching Darth Vader about to lead his minions into battle. Fortunately my shift (nights) was not blessed with an abundance of Sisters. The technicians worked for the most part in pairs and unsupervised.

My shift partner, Peter Weston, an early proponent of medical marijuana and enthusiastic supporter of all things cannabis, was able to drift through the long, lonely hours of the night playing his guitar and smoking Marlboros. Between scrubbing loads of mucus-encrusted equipment (while listening to Pink Floyd's *Dark Side of the Moon*), Peter was content to contemplate the deeper things of life... things like where we came from and what man's purpose is, (if any). Things we loved to debate—the agnostic vs. the believer.

One of his favorite topics, though, was discussing the countless benefits of using recreational marijuana. If Peter wasn't smoking it, he was talking about smoking it, and when he wasn't talking about smoking it, he was often eating it. Brownies were his specialty.

One night he mentioned that he had recently perfected a brownie recipe, and that I should come over to his place so we could play guitars, listen to music, and enjoy some. Naturally this was *before* informing me that brownies were his preferred method of ingesting controlled substances. Assuming Peter had simply developed yet another life interest, that of cooking, and unaware of the secret ingredient, I agreed to stop by the following Saturday when we were scheduled off.

He smiled and quietly declared, "*Nobody* can make a brownie like I can Greg. It's all about the ingredients. *Quality* ingredients," he emphasized. "Come by around 8:00 then?"

PERMISSION TO OBSERVE

*   *   *

Late that Saturday night at Peter's apartment with Pink Floyd's haunting *Shine on You Crazy Diamond* thundering in the background, he proudly appeared from the kitchen with a large, badly dented brownie pan. As he carefully divided the batch and handed me a generous (double) portion, we sat down on the sofa, smiled at each other, and began nibbling.

I don't recall much beyond that. One thing I do remember is that I had an impossible time trying *not* to laugh. Like a giddy child being held and tickled, I thought *everything* Peter said was hysterical. Even the slightest mention of something as sobering as having recently lost a relative to illness had me on the floor.

The following Monday when we reported to work, Peter was noticeably quiet the first couple of hours. I didn't push it, but I knew I'd worn out my welcome Saturday night. More important, I realized I'd lost all hope of ever getting another one of those delightful brownies.

*   *   *

There were other colorful characters on staff. One in particular (a nun) was especially curious. She must have been close to ninety at the time, yet was no larger than a ten year old. We called her Sister Eeg, mainly because of the striking resemblance she bore to *Igor*, the hunch-backed lab assistant in *Frankenstein*.

Possessing a generous Dowager's hump on her right shoulder and blind in one eye, Sister Eeg never missed a night. She would show up wearing a black eye patch while cocking her head in a nervous twitch much like a praying mantis. Apparently this behavior was due to her limited vision.

Even though the top of her cap barely reached five feet, she was an impish terror—able to intimidate the pants off anyone who crossed her. The Medical Director and Chief of Staff vowed never to confront her. If she happened to be walking down the hall during the day (she must have *never* slept), groups of employees would part like the Red Sea as she shuffled toward wherever it was she was going.

Sister Eeg worked the night shift, roaming the blackened patient corridors seemingly lost in thought and in desperate need of something. Each evening around midnight, she would wander down the halls, breathing heavily and chattering some nonsense about a lost soul as she aimed her six-volt industrial-strength flashlight in each room, waking nearly every patient.

"Not in here," she'd mumble. "Not here either."

We quickly learned to turn our heads when we saw her coming. Otherwise, we were blinded by the intense white beam. The other nuns said she was doing her rounds and we should ignore her. The general consensus was that she was just plain nuts. I don't know if she ever found what or who she was looking for, but I admired her spunk.

*   *   *

Near the end of each shift, around six in the morning, Peter and I looked forward to finishing our paperwork, tying up loose ends and making sure everything was ready for the incoming day crew.

We would then make a bee-line for the freight elevator. Destination—sixth floor waiting room, north end of the building. Reason—to watch the sun rise and solve the problems of the world. We had some of the most profound conversations during those hours before heading to the cafeteria for our daily bread—bacon and eggs.

One morning, as we sipped hot coffee and yawned, we looked out over the waking city and noticed something different. More police cars than usual. A series of city patrol cars had begun slowly streaming down the east side of the building on the main thoroughfare. And then, two patrol units approached from the south, about to cross the closest major intersection. The residential section west of the hospital also had a unit creeping toward the building.

It was obvious. St. Bart's was being surrounded.

The police cars kept moving past the hospital almost at a crawl, occasionally slowing to a stop. Wondering what was going on (but too tired to care), we returned to the department, signed out, and headed to the ER doors directly across from the parking lot.

As we passed through the doorway, we asked the night shift guard, Rayford Wallace ('Rayf' for short) if he had heard what was going on. Rayf had an old police radio he liked listening to while he manned his post. This gave him the insider's scoop and allowed him the luxury of boasting that he knew more about the pulse of the city than any of the folks he worked with. He only had pieces of information but from what he'd gathered, an escaped convict was likely in the area and police were on the lookout.

Having worked nights for twenty years, Rayf was a familiar face at St. Bart's. With his radio by his side and warm personality, he was considered a prime source of gossip for anyone interested in listening. Each person coming to the emergency room for treatment was greeted with a grin as wide as the Cleveland Indians' mascot and enough sparkle for *two* mouths. Stretched tight over the rows of teeth, Rayf's lips barely moved when he nodded and directed patients to the triage area. "Welcome to St. Bart's where we hep' you git well," was his standard greeting.

On the small, splintered desk next to Rayf's chair rested a large silver book with three thin gummy lines running the length of the cover, and fine strands of hair-like threads hanging from the edge. It was Rayf's Bible, carefully and lovingly covered in duct tape. Rayf opened his good book so often that it was polished to a bright sheen, the gold trim having worn away years ago while the pages remained diaper-soft.

He read during his lunch break and never missed a night. He was also famous for his unusually animated belly laugh. You couldn't help but notice, and it was contagious. He would begin chuckling slowly while his enormous gut began to ride up and down. With each breath the volume grew until he would finally throw his head back in a roar, filling the room with raucous laughter—all while baring those perfect teeth.

* * *

That morning, as we approached the ER doors, Rayf spotted us coming down the hall. Grinning full-face he said, "Better scoot on out to yo cars boys," he warned. "Don't let that boogeyman git you. He on the loose!" Then the belly would start. We would nod, yawn, thank Rayf for his concern, and start backing out the doors—trying to make the break like every other sleepy morning.

Rayf had an annoying talent for stretching five simple words like "It was slow last night" into a half hour description. Neither of us was in the mood, since we had been insanely busy for the past eight hours; three patients with breathing treatments every two hours; oxygen and ventilator rounds in the ICU, one cardiac arrest (which threw everything off), and two loads of dirty equipment left over from the evening shift.

No surprise though. The moon would be full again the next night, and you learned to expect the worst during a full moon. Like Rayf often said, "Be kerful, dem loonies will be out!" We just wanted to go home. I had one thought—get through the police dragnet, or whatever it was, and get to bed.

* * *

Returning the following night, I knew Rayf was scheduled off, so I wouldn't be able to get the full story on the police business until I checked in with the evening shift crew. As soon as I walked through the department doors and blindly made my way through the pillar of cloud, multiple voices peppered me with versions of the same question, *"Did you hear what happened after you left this morning?"* Apparently, the police search had turned into a full-blown manhunt with the chase climaxing in a pool of blood on the front steps of St. Bartholomew Hospital.

The details involved a 26 year-old drug dealer arrested earlier in the day who was being transported from one of the nearby district stations to the city work house. Somehow, he had managed to break free of his handcuffs, scuffle with at least one officer, and commandeer a patrol car for his escape. All units had been put on high alert as the suspect headed east toward the river and the Illinois state line.

As Val, the evening shift technician who I was relieving, filled me in on what had happened that morning, I thought about where I might have been had I lingered a few minutes after breakfast. As it turned out, during his flight toward East St. Louis, the escapee had taken an unexpected detour south, toward the hospital at high speed. It was later determined that he had been listening to the radio dispatcher and was able to route his escape based on the broadcast information. Although the police had a system in place for confidentiality in these situations (by systematically switching to other radio frequencies), the suspect was able to follow the pattern of channel switches and elude capture.

His mistake was when he accelerated as he approached the hospital grounds. Losing control, he skidded into a Bi-State bus sign at the southeast corner of the parking lot—the momentum carrying him into the surrounding eight foot chain link fence where the car finally came to rest, one wheel still spinning.

With the squad car bouncing like a giant bug in a spider web, the man tumbled out and sprinted along the front edge of the property straight toward the hospital's main entrance, and Rayf, who had been listening to the dispatcher on his radio. Having positioned himself just inside the main entrance, Rayf was waiting, prepared to defend his beloved St. Bartholomew.

No one understood exactly why the suspect suddenly chose to run across the sprawling lawn toward the main entrance of the hospital. We'll probably never know. Maybe he thought he could duck inside unnoticed and head toward the laundry or some other hiding hole, like the morgue.

By the time he crossed the dew-covered grass, leaped up the three steps, and landed in the shadow of the giant crucifix overhead—he was immediately greeted by a wide, toothy grin.

*　*　*

Witnesses watching from a distance didn't know what to make of the exchange between the men. Apparently a moment or two had passed as the pair began sizing each other up. They seemed to know one another. From witness information later provided, the first to react was Rayf. In response to something said or gestured by the suspect, Rayf had reached up with both hands to grab the suspect by his shoulders, an uncommon and ineffective method of restraint. This split second of vulnerability was all the intruder needed.

Since the escapee was left-handed, and Rayf was right-handed, the gun was holstered on the guard's right hip. Contract security guards, at the time, were equipped with the standard police-issue .38 caliber six-shot revolver. The gun would have been secured in a straight laced holster, with a simple leather flap and metal snap.

A cinch to withdraw.

As soon as a grab was possible, the suspect wrenched the .38 out of its cradle, raised it and fired a single shot into Rayf's throat. Since the subject was a few inches shorter, it allowed him the opportunity to fire at a slight upward angle, through the bottom of the jaw and out the base of Rayf's skull... a shot the police later termed a "through and through." The shell created a tunnel of destruction through the cerebellum at the base of the skull. The path had instantly obliterated the central nervous system knocking out Rayf's respiratory drive. He was essentially dead by the time he hit the concrete.

Within an hour, police had re-captured the suspect (now shooter) and returned him to the station for booking. Ultimately, the perpetrator would face the maximum charge... *murder in the first degree*. By taking possession of the firearm, he caused the death of another while in the commission of a felony. In the state of Missouri, that immediately becomes a capital offense punishable by death.

* * *

The main lobby of St. Bartholomew had not been used as a patient reception area for some time. All access to the hospital had been rerouted through the Emergency Room years earlier in the hope of reducing traffic and noise since the Sisters resided on the second floor.

The Chapel, just inside the main atrium, was now cordoned off with yellow crime scene tape. A three-foot statue of Christ with outstretched arms and mounted on a pedestal watched quietly from one corner. The nuns would still be allowed to attend Mass. They had insisted.

By the end of that awful day, the Sisters had dutifully cleaned the spilled blood and tissue fragments as best they could, yet a sizeable stain remained on the top step. The shooter had tossed the gun alongside the building in the bushes, which was recovered. The bullet was never found.

* * *

Once Peter and I heard the full story, we realized we had to visit the scene. Others in the department shared our grim curiosity and had satisfied their own earlier in the day. That night, the hallways were dark as usual. But this time it was different. There was an eerie heaviness in the air that caused feelings of attraction and repulsion as we walked the last corridor.

Nearing the Chapel vestibule, we saw the yellow tape stretched across the beautifully carved, arched doors trimmed in stained glass. The air was thick with the smell of old wax and lemon disinfectant. The crime scene strips looked out of place, especially since nothing really had been disturbed on the inside. It had all happened outside, beneath the cross that had somehow now been defiled.

Lifting the edge of the tape, we silently crossed the line to get a clear view of the outside step through the glass. There was just enough light coming from the streetlamps, passing cars, and of course... the full moon.

Although the nuns had done their best to remove any signs of struggle, the unmistakable red oval stain had been sealed into the pores of concrete and brick. It would require power washing to remove it.

That's all that was left of Rayf. It was hard to take my eyes off that print. The spilled liquid represented life— Rayf's life—someone who had cared enough to risk his own for others.

But it was all wrong.

The spot wasn't supposed to be there and my mind couldn't wrap itself around the thought of such a violent crime and what Rayf had sacrificed—all in a place where the very sound of a heartbeat is considered precious, honorable, and priceless.

* * *

We stood there for what must have been a full minute. But it was a holy minute—and holy ground. Not because it happened to be at the entrance of a Catholic hospital or because the Chapel was near. It was holy ground because it had become the threshold of eternity for a friend.

Permission to Observe

Peter and I made our way slowly back to the basement. Seated at the long department desk, we silently divided the night's work and gathered up our supplies.

We walked to the elevator that led to the patient rooms... toward the land of beating hearts.

—Chapter 3—

Deliveries

*"What is better than presence of mind in a railway accident?
... absence of body"*

Punch, 1849 British humor magazine

PERMISSION TO OBSERVE

A few miles from St. Bartholomew lay the 1293-acre paradise of St. Louis—Forest Park. With its beautiful gardens, fountains, and trails, the park provides a peaceful respite from the chaos of no less than six busy medical centers, some within walking distance. The park is also home to such prestigious institutions as the St. Louis Art Museum, the St. Louis Zoo, and The Muny Opera—a seasonal outdoor theater which has played host to such notables as Bob Hope, Tony Randall, and Phyllis Diller.

Nearby is the magnificent Metropolitan Medical Center complex, a group of research, treatment, and educational facilities providing knowledge and care for virtually any ailment found in the textbooks—and many that are not.

One hospital within the group was a pioneer of off-site care, having opened one of the first dispensaries in the city. There, a young physician from the Johns Hopkins Medical School became the first surgeon in St. Louis to use rubber gloves while operating. These two strategies combined served as a powerful catalyst, altering the course of medicine forever.

* * *

Aside from being born at Metropolitan, I knew little of the rich history of the hospital and the influence it had on the community. I can remember my mother taking me to the Met for the treatment of various childhood diseases and injuries. I never concerned myself with the hospital's proximity to the historic Chase Park Plaza Hotel, then, one of the tallest buildings in the area.

The top floor of the hotel contained the studios of a local TV station, KPLR, which provided great local programming like the "Captain 11 Show" featuring cartoons, games, and most notably—regular episodes of *The Three Stooges*. Mothers cringed every day at 3:30 when they heard the inane theme music along with the blow of the Captain's riverboat horn.

Toward the end of the show's run, the Captain was able to book the Stooges as live studio guests. By that time, Curley was dead and Joe had taken his place. They looked fat, old, and terribly wrinkled—but they were still heroes to kids my age. Whenever we passed the Chase on our way to the hospital, I would spin around on the back seat of our 1959 Nash Rambler (the one the wheel fell off—twice), prop my knees on the green-plaid vinyl back seat, and crane my neck toward the top of the rear windshield to see if I could get a glimpse of the Captain or the Stooges through the studio's tinted windows. I never did.

*   *   *

Fresh out of high school, I got a job at a local gas station while going to college. The Phillips 66 in Jennings had been bought by twin brothers,—ex-hippies with thick mustaches and Beatle haircuts who swore they were at Woodstock (but never could produce ticket stubs). I was eighteen and determined to learn my new three-in-one role of husband, father, and son-in-law.

Nervous about all the responsibilities in my world, I was restless and itching to get started working in healthcare. The Metropolitan Medical Center afforded me just the opportunity, even before I completed formal training in Respiratory Therapy.

Answering an ad in the Post-Dispatch one weekend, I was invited to come in the following week to interview with Metropolitan's new Nursing Service Administrator, Mr. Harris, a thin, pipe-smoking wire-rimmed nerd. Harris sported a thick mustache and was fond of using the pipe's mouthpiece as his pointer—touching anything within reach. Desktops, paperwork, equipment, employees... I once saw him tap a nurse on the shoulder to get her attention while ashes tumbled out, sprinkling her uniform with hot tobacco dust. It didn't appear to alarm her when he did it. He was simply thought to be eccentric. Besides, he could fire you on the spot.

Permission to Observe

The job I interviewed for was a newly created role as a Transport Orderly. There were actually four positions to be filled, which would provide sixteen hours of daily coverage for the nursing department in an extremely busy facility. I was hired with two young inner-city residents named Lawrence and Randall, along with a guy from Nicaragua named Juan. I'm not sure how Juan was able to get through the interview process. His command of English was weak at best. Nearly everything he said needed repeating, and there was often an uncomfortably long silence after the *second* attempt, because the brain required sufficient time to decipher what was just uttered (twice). To make matters worse, he had poor eyesight and wore lenses so thick, all you could see were blurry dark circles. There was little eye contact which made basic communication all the more challenging.

On one occasion, the four of us were sitting in the break room waiting for the afternoon shift change. Juan was particularly talkative as he tried to describe the pitiful living conditions in his small Central American village. Most of the other employees in the room just stared at him while he rambled on, holding his hands a full foot apart to illustrate the size of the nightly visitors that plagued his house, referring to them as "glate beeg cock-a-roaches." By the time he finished sharing but one of his many plights, I would already be headed out the door to start my rounds.

*   *   *

Specimen rounds were to be done throughout the shift, beginning on the even hours. All of the floors were split between two orderlies, with each complete cycle taking just over an hour. Depending on the volume and types of samples to be collected, we often had little time for other activities.

I used a bulky, squeaking metal cart I heaved from division to division, stopping at the nursing stations and working my way down from the ninth floor—ending up in the basement where the labs were located. Since the staff could easily hear the squeaks coming from the far end of the hall, the samples were usually assembled on the counter along with the requisitions, ready for pickup and delivery.

The treks in search of blood vials, urine-filled plastic cups (which often leaked), stool samples (in the same type of leaky cup), or some other unidentified mass, were often interrupted by the beeping of a pager, a small rectangular receiver not much bigger than a Pez dispenser.

One of us was required to carry it at all times and respond immediately. The beeper had a tiny square button on the side near the top where the speaker was. Once sounded, you had to hold the unit up, burying it in your ear while depressing the button, and listening to the lively voice of your superior, doubtlessly calling to give instructions for an urgent task. There was so much static and interference it sounded like the caller was standing in a hurricane.

Normally, the portable pager would be viewed as a convenient and efficient communication tool. Unless, of course, the caller happened to be Miss Betty, one of the evening shift nursing supervisors who wielded far too much clout in the organization. Betty was a graduate (and faculty member) of the Metropolitan Medical Center School of Nursing and felt that her particular calling was to keep the lowly nursing department employees (like orderlies) ever alert.

One of her favorite tactics was to call the orderly's pager, wait for the tone, and say something like, "Please report to the fifth floor nursing station, we have a patient about to jump from a window," or "Please return the fecal sample you just picked up in ICU, the patient has more."

*   *   *

Her shining moment came one Sunday night when, in the middle of rounds, the familiar voice crackled over the pager, "We have an oxygen-related fire here in the SICU—

Get here STAT!" Upon arrival in the unit, neither my co-worker Lawrence, nor I could detect the slightest trace of smoke—only the shoulders of Betty rising and falling as she chuckled with another supervisor. "We just wanted to see how quickly you two knuckleheads would respond," laughed Betty. "There is no fire."

It occurred to me later that if there truly had been a fire—why would she page *us* and not the fire department? So my reaction was to inform Mr. Harris the next morning of these little "tests" she was so fond of administering.

It became clear when I shared the information that he didn't like Miss Betty either. Soon after, she was transferred to the day shift and told to take a break from her unorthodox training style. Short of firing her, it was the only way he could control her since she happened to be a *very* close friend of the hospital President.

* * *

Part of my job as Transport Orderly included moving patients at the whim of nursing. This often meant lifting a post-op patient from a chair to bed or perhaps from wheelchair to exam table while the nurse more than likely slipped around the corner for a quick smoke.

Another part of the job was providing the patent's final elevator ride to the basement morgue. For that reason we were issued a specially-designed stretcher with a removable canvas canopy that allowed us to move a body through the halls virtually unnoticed.

It gave the appearance of a vacant stretcher being rolled to a room for a routine transport. Hidden beneath the tarp, however, was a rectangular stainless steel tray with a raised, forty-five degree lip around the edge. Once the tray, referred to by my fellow orderlies as "the cheeseboard," was cranked to a height level with the bed, the body could be pulled across the lip and maneuvered into the tray using the under sheet. It was then simply a matter of tightly tucking any dangling limbs into the shroud, lowering the cheeseboard, popping the lid back on—and off you'd go.

In the course of our duties, the paths of orderlies would occasionally cross—one pushing the noisy specimen cart, the other a loaded morgue cart. Having spied each other at opposite ends of the hall, we would pause to make eye contact, firm our grips, and race to see who could get to the elevator button first. Nursing tended to frown on this practice.

When wheeling an 'occupied' morgue stretcher into the cramped, dark, service elevator, people who knew what lay beneath the stained beige cover would react in a variety of ways. I was astonished at the superstitious behavior of some of the nurse aides when faced with a death.

Some would stare at the top surface, perhaps pensively wondering what befell the individual. If there were no visitors riding the service elevator with us (the main elevators were so slow that visitors were often directed to use the service elevators), we would freely discuss the cause of death and circumstances.

Other staff on the elevator, however, would see me happily whistling as I rolled in through the doors, and would promptly exit the elevator, hugging the walls with splayed fingers like tree frogs as they turned to the stairs. "I ain't takin' *this* bus—no way no how," and "Now just let me scoot on outa here," seemed to be common reactions.

For the most part, the deaths occurring on the general care patient floors were simply age or heart-related. No trauma, no surgery, no gore. Just... time's up. One such death and subsequent transport, however, became one of the most talked about at Metropolitan. Once again, our leader, Mr. Harris, was able to share the limelight as a result of his staff's uncanny knack for incompetence.

*　　*　　*

PERMISSION TO OBSERVE

It happened on a Sunday. My two inner-city colleagues, Lawrence and Randall, were scheduled to work the day shift, and would need to pick up a body on the fourth floor—a 79 year old female named Lily Bledsoe who had suffered a fatal heart attack. Lily was a complicated southern lady, full of charm, grace and venom. I got to know her because her physician had ordered several tests which required being transported to multiple locations over the course of a few days. We would share small talk during these excursions and developed a genuine friendship.

She preferred to be called Miss Lily, and did most of the talking. That was a relief since I was usually concentrating on catching my breath while wheeling the 260-pound patient with one hand and struggling to carry (and not drop) her oxygen tank with the other. Apparently, the hospital's financial director didn't see the need to equip wheel chairs with oxygen cylinder brackets. Far too costly.

Miss Lily told me she was a three pack-a-day smoker, which is why she had to use oxygen. She wore the nasal cannula continuously throughout the day and night. Whenever I showed up at her door with a wheelchair I would first have to hoist the small (but cumbersome) sixteen-pound portable tank in one hand and strain to push her chair, all the while listening to rambling tales of oak-lined plantations, moss-strewn trees, and her favorite beverage—a tumbler of Jack Daniels with a single ice cube. "Now one itty-bitty cube is all you need darlin'," she'd drawl.

It was the itty-bitty pleasures of her life, along with morbid obesity that made Miss Lily a ticking time bomb.

When I left work Friday night, she was failing. Her blood gas report indicated that she was not getting enough oxygen, despite an order for a much higher flow delivered through the face mask they had switched her to. Worse, she

34

was becoming increasingly congested and drifted in a semi-conscious state.

In the early morning hours on Sunday, Miss Lily finally succumbed to her long battle with COPD (chronic obstructive pulmonary disease), and died of a massive heart attack. The staff had reluctantly called a code but the outcome was obvious. The continuous, checkered strip of paper being spit out of the bedside ECG machine clearly indicated that her heart was beyond saving. Only a small, ocean-wave pattern appeared. No spikes, no beats, no life. "That's it. I'm calling it," the night resident had declared.

The time was noted at 4:12 a.m.

Staff immediately began the dispassionate disconnecting process (which always made me uncomfortable), freeing Miss Lily from tubes, wires, tape, and monitors. The required paperwork, along with assembling the chart was a monumental chore in itself. It often took an hour or more. Once the documentation was complete and Miss Lily was freed from all worldly ties, she would be toe-tagged, swaddled in the bed sheet, and ready for the trip to the morgue.

For a death during the early morning hours, the body would typically be held in the patient's room until the day shift orderlies reported to work at 6:00 a.m. (when Lawrence and Randall happened to be scheduled). They could then make the delivery a priority—their first task of the day. But a three to four hour delay in getting a body to the morgue tended to make someone like Miss Lilly stubborn and impatient, even in death.

*　*　*

There are so many rapid changes set in motion at the time of death and onset of decay that the deceased may become livelier than the living. Ironically, within minutes of the final heart beat, blood continues to move and seeks its new home by pooling in the lowest part of the body. This causes the skin in those areas to turn a deep shade of purple-red, becoming discolored by a process called *livor mortis* or what embalmers term 'postmortem stain.' Sometime later, the blood wearies of its years of constant travel and becomes fixed, never to leave the area. Skin also follows the tug of gravity creating new (sometimes unnatural) shapes and contours which funeral directors find challenging.

After a few hours *rigor mortis* takes its turn in the process. This increasing stiffness normally begins with the eyelids, jaw, neck, and ultimately spreads to the remaining muscles and organs. The cooling of the body, *algor mortis,* not surprisingly, is accelerated in a cold environment—one like that of a morgue refrigerator. So after it's all said and done, once prepped and positioned for viewing, old Aunt Clara may not end up looking much like old Aunt Clara.

A mortician can only do so much.

*   *   *

Lawrence and Randall were already having problems that day. They had both overslept, missing the 5:20 a.m. bus. By the time they arrived and made their way to the nursing office for assignments, they were greeted with a scowl and tongue-lashing from the receptionist, Helen, a nurse who had thankfully retired from direct patient care—but loved to bark orders like a drill sergeant.

"It's about time," she said. "Get your pager and your sorry asses to the fourth floor nursing station. Don't bother with the first set of specimen rounds. They can wait," she said. "The funeral home will be here soon and that body needs to be where they can get it." She paused, gave a dramatic sigh and asked, "Now, what's keeping you?" Helen loved her job.

The unfortunate thing was that neither orderly had ever performed a body pick-up and transport. Miss Lily would be the first—and last.

Leaving the nursing office, the orderlies had reluctantly located the storage closet where the morgue stretcher was kept. As they began stumbling through the piles of equipment, they spied the stretcher buried under stacks of old dented bed pans that formed a large, shiny pyramid. After repeatedly trying to free-up the wheels that had become wedged between catheter cases and admission kits, they successfully managed to waste another thirty minutes.

This gave Miss Lily an opportunity to stiffen up a bit more.

With only a small wattage bulb overhead, the two orderlies stumbled through the clutter like blindfolded prisoners, slowing the process even more. Both dreaded what they had to do, but neither would speak. They shared similar superstitions and wanted to be nowhere near the corpse, let alone have to touch it. Had a bus been scheduled to stop at the hospital entrance at that moment, the two of them would have hopped aboard, gladly paying *triple* fare for a ride anywhere.

There was no turning back now. Admitting was ready to fill the soon-vacant bed, while Helen impatiently waited for the go-ahead call letting her know the patient had been removed and that the room had been properly turned over. She decided to page the boneheads to find out why it was taking so insufferably long to do such a simple task.

At the unexpected beep of the pager in his pocket, Lawrence jerked just as they had wrestled the stretcher free. Knocking down the bed pan pyramid and shattering a glass I.V. bottle perched on a shelf, he yelped "Shee-it man!" as the cold saline splashed and quickly soaked his pants.

"*Now w*hat are we 'sposed to do?" He looked at Randall who was shaking his head and softly mumbling something about the Lord Jesus.

*   *   *

Realizing they had no choice, they began pushing the stretcher down the hall toward Lily's room. They knew which one it was, since no one was in the immediate area and hers was the only door closed with the tell-tale empty flip chart slot mounted beside the door. Lily's family stayed home to make funeral arrangements.

An LPN on duty at the nurse station watched as the two orderlies approached Lily's room. She later told her supervisor what she had seen. "Those idiots," she said. "They actually *knocked* on the door of a dead patient's private room. I couldn't believe it."

To complicate things, the boys hadn't been keen on note-taking during employee orientation. That's when they were supposedly trained on the proper use of the stretcher. Had they paid attention in class, they would have remembered that the foot end was equipped with a hand crank which allowed the user to raise or lower the entire tray to match the exact height of the bed, thereby making the transfer of the body relatively easy. In the neutral transport position however, the tray would be at its lowest point and the crank would be hidden underneath.

This made a difference of about eighteen inches, or, in Miss Lily's case, all the difference in the world. It is also likely that they had lost all manner of common sense by the time they finally tip-toed into her room. When the two mustered the courage to look at the enormous mummy-like mound lying motionless and tightly wrapped in the sheet, they were in obvious agreement that faster is better.

Once they had parallel-parked the stretcher next to the bed, lifted off the canvas top with four Parkinson-like hands, and noticed the low position of the tray, they realized there was a serious problem.

At first they thought it would be easy enough to let the body slide over the edge of the mattress, starting from the head and working its way down to the legs and feet. Like a slow-motion water fall, or an Olympic high jumper sailing softly over the bar. The body would hug the edge of the bed and follow the natural path of descent.

But then, there was that pesky rigor problem.

The firming stages had produced a level of rigidity in Miss Lily that quickly disqualified option one. So the only thing the orderlies could think of was to line the tray with several pillows, pull the body slowly, and hope for the best.

* * *

Once they had positioned themselves along the far side of the stretcher, reaching across the tray, they grasped the sheet and began to pull, being ever-so-careful not to touch the thing inside. Grunting and cursing as Miss Lily's enormous form had reached the edge of the mattress, the orderlies realized that her weight had suddenly become a factor. With the mattress edge starting to flatten, a sudden shift and roll had begun that was unstoppable. Her body turned as the sheet simultaneously unraveled. Then, briefly facing the two orderlies for a split second before plummeting into the tray, Miss Lily released an explosive belch loud enough to be heard at the station.

It was the gaseous lion-like roar that made Randall jump, causing him to trip backward, accidently pulling one of the tray pillows with him. The sheet wrapped around the body had come loose while momentum and gravity took over. They both watched Miss Lily's descent as if in slow motion—right along with their careers.

She ended up face down, bouncing in the center of the tray with arms spread wide in a final sky-dive pose. Once she had landed, it was all the orderlies could do to reposition her arms and legs, tucking them back in place and rewrapping the sheet. After wiping the sweat and taking a collective breath, they composed themselves enough to wheel Miss Lily out the door. It was at that moment that one of them looked down and noticed the handle crank dangling. *Now* they remembered.

The handle discovery actually provided some relief. They realized that once they made it to the morgue's refrigerator door, the crank would allow them to ratchet the cheeseboard up high enough to meet the level of the slide-out refrigerator tray. So all they had to do then was pull the wrapped mass straight across the tray's edge and be done with it, never once thinking to flip Miss Lily onto her *back* as the livor, rigor, and algor effects all did their magic.

* * *

When she was claimed by the funeral home, hospital administration was promptly contacted by the funeral director, informing them that the method of physical transfer of the patient from her room to the morgue had somehow caused *"Postmortem artifacts with significant facial trauma and subsequent contortion of certain features,"* and that the family would have to be advised of the condition of the body. Apparently, Miss Lily now sported a slight crook in her nose—which now rested just under her left eye.

There was only so much a mortician could do.

* * *

The next day I clocked-in at my regular time. When I picked up the pager from the nursing office, I was instructed to report immediately to Mr. Harris' office. He told me what had happened and that replacements for Lawrence and Randall would soon be hired. After hearing the whole sorry story from Lawrence earlier in the day, it was only the *second* time in his management career that Mr. Harris recalled having to fire someone over the phone.

Randall was his first.

* * *

Sometime later there were rumblings of legal action by the family, that Miss Lily's children were incensed by the "inept and disrespectful handling" of their mother's body, and rightfully so.

The painful truth though, is that as long as people are involved in the process, shortcomings, weakness, and miserable failures are bound to occur at some stage. Not necessarily prevail—but they *will* occur. Imperfection is unavoidable.

Just ask Miss Lily.

* * *

I shared the story of Miss Lily with my older brother several years ago. He has a reputation of keen insight with an unusual ability to verbalize some of the more profound topics related to the human condition, albeit in a curmudgeonly style.

He has pondered the origin of the universe, contemplated the frailty of human nature, reflected on the creation of man, and weighed the realm of human intelligence by concluding the following:

"If God would have rested on the *sixth* day (when man was made) instead of the seventh—we wouldn't have all these problems."

Discovery

—Chapter 4—

A Calling

"People don't choose their careers;
They are engulfed by them"

John Dos Pasos,
New York Times, 1959

Permission to Observe

If asked what influenced me to consider a healthcare career in the first place, a couple of things come to mind. One would have to be a photograph on the glossy recruiting brochure I saw one day in high school. The image of a Respiratory Therapist (back then, Inhalation Therapist) performing CPR on a victim was dramatic, and from a college recruiter's standpoint—darned effective. I had never heard of the profession and had no idea what they did. But when I saw that picture, I was hooked.

Commonly referred to as "bagging" (manually breathing for the victim), the central theme of the image was truly the stuff of life and death. The rescuer was shown kneeling behind the head of an unconscious victim. With the fingers of her left hand curled along the edge of the jaw, she squeezed a football-shaped resuscitator bag using her right hand—all with the strength, poise, and confidence of a professional athlete.

Even earlier in life, I was addicted to the TV medical drama, *Ben Casey.* I couldn't wait to see each weekly episode with Vincent Edwards playing the part of Dr. Casey—an easy-going, but tough physician whose gentle bedside manner often shifted to explosive anger when crossed by co-workers or superiors. This made the character both lovable and detestable. The fact that he was a rebel appealed to me.

For example, his refusal to button the collar of his smock at the insistence of his frizzy-headed superior, Dr. Zorba, made me yearn for the kind of job where I could save lives, scream at subordinates, snub my superiors, and dress how I pleased. I still remember the dramatic camera close-up during the show's opening sequence, when a hand slowly drew five symbols vertically on a chalk-board as the scratchy-voiced Sam Jaffe would narrate:

"Man... Woman... Birth... Death... Infinity!"

GREGORY R. FROST, RRT

Despite the show's popularity, my friends expressed little interest in career medicine. Firemen, policemen, soldiers and the like were far more appealing to young testosterone-fueled boys. But for me, that early dream of white coats, sparkly stethoscopes, and mysterious x-rays later became a reality—working as a transport orderly at Metropolitan Medical Center in one of the city's highest crime areas. Despite questionable safety, other risks existed like daily exposure to every kind of body fluid and infectious disease imaginable, being subject to the condescending attitudes and egos of childish professionals, and the toll the whole thing takes on a person in that environment day after day. The main casualty of war for the healthcare worker lurked everywhere—the habitual stress of managing relationships, illness, death, and loss.

Yet, the whole idea held an irresistible allure. This attraction was confirmed the day I had a chance to snap on a pair of vinyl gloves and help with what might be the most extraordinary job in the hospital—the autopsy assistant.

* * *

Phillip, Metropolitan's sole morgue attendant, was arguably gay. Short, thin, and near retirement, he had greasy, badly combed salt and pepper hair, wore thick black-rimmed glasses, and was loosely draped in a worn grey lab coat with several patches. His unmistakable body language was dramatically effeminate. With left hand swinging in wide arcs as his right hand rested firmly on his hip, he paraded down the hall from the coffee stand to the stairwell, smiling and nodding at passers-by like a beauty contestant waiting to be crowned.

Instead of the social interaction most of us need in stress-filled jobs, Phillip took great pride in his craft as a loner. Anything outside his department held little interest for him. Rarely seen upstairs, he performed all aspects of his job with complete devotion and a clear sense of servitude.

Phillip loved the lifeless bodies, and preferred the intimacy and calm of the two-room windowless morgue to anything on the patient floors.

To him, the dead became his friends. He would talk to them, sing or hum songs as he carefully separated the tissues, letting them know what he was about to do. He even enjoyed his lunch there.

It was not unusual to walk into the morgue around mid-day and find Phillip seated at his matching grey metal desk that would be stacked with pathology reports, piles of unopened mail, syringes (some with needles attached), and three or four half-empty bottles of Yoo-Hoo chocolate soda. His favorite lunch consisted of a can of sardines, some crackers, and a pack of Twinkies. He enjoyed every bite, just within arm's reach of his newest acquaintances.

Since I was his prime supplier of customers, we got to know each other. Having company while he worked was always a bonus for Phillip, which is how I got the invitation one day to assist him.

* * *

He had just cracked the chest of a man I had delivered the night before. An afternoon post-mortem was required, since the cause of death was possibly crime-related. I had just left specimen samples at the lab next door, and stuck my head in to say hello when I saw Phillip lift the entire front section of the ribs cage off the man's torso, like the lid of a Weber kettle. I was astounded by what I saw for the first time—the inside of the human body, a compact assortment of warm colors, smooth bubbly textures, and glistening surfaces, along with a never before experienced odor that was warm, musty, and coppery.

I leaned further in and asked for permission to observe. Phillip gave me a wink that made me more than a bit uncomfortable, saying, "Absolutely you can, Gregory. Here... put these gloves on."

I hated when he called me Gregory.

He held a box of disposable gloves within reach then quickly returned to his work. As I fumbled with each glove, Phillip was lost in his own little world, humming softly (this time a hymn) as he sliced, sawed, chipped, and severed the man to bits. He took his craft seriously.

His supervisor was a young pathologist from the Philippines named Dr. Amelda Montez. He always referred to her as 'Mel' but as infrequently as I saw her, she was Dr. Montez to me. She was short, had a thick accent and was eight months pregnant. With her swollen belly she could barely examine the freshly-gutted cavities and was often forced to use a stepstool kept under the dissection table.

I watched as she slid the stool out with one foot, steadied herself as she stepped up and then plunged her hands into the upper right section of the dead man's gaping man-made hole. Concentrating on her search, she quickly located the liver. After freeing it from its tough, fibrous sheath, she severed the lobes from their main anchor—the cluster of tubes merging on the under-side that create the common bile duct, the path leading to the gall bladder. She held up the organ with both hands to examine the surface, squeezed a few times, and began sniffing various areas in search of faint traces of ammonia or alcohol. Satisfied, she then plopped it in the scale which hung just above John Doe's feet. It was the same kind of scale my mom used to weigh her vegetables at Kroger, which made me wonder what a human liver might actually be worth.

I always considered human organs and tissues, along with their respective functions, as perfectly designed and priceless. Farther down my career path, however, I would learn some disturbing facts about the transplant industry which I would one day join. Not all organs are created equal, nor are they priceless.

Dr. Montez scooped out the three-pound liver from the steel pan, still dripping yellow-green bile and held the slippery mass next to her apron. She reached across the table and picked up one of her favorite tools, a ten-inch carving blade with a wooden handle. As she began slowly and carefully sectioning the main lobes of the liver like a fresh summer tomato, there was something surreal about it. As she cradled the organ next to her pregnant belly, the only thing separating the dead tissue from the baby's living tissue was a layer of skin. In a way, the child was confronting death for the very first time, with only a thin wall of protective flesh and blood separating the two.

Dr. Montez learned from Phillip that I would soon begin college with the hope of working as a healthcare professional. She assumed it was nursing. When I told her that I had enrolled in the Cardiopulmonary Technology program, she asked if the coursework included Respiratory Therapy (I suspect she already knew the answer). When I told her that it was, in fact, my major she smiled and said in a thick Southeast Asian accent, "I show you trick boy. You not forget dis... k?"

On a rusty nail just above the dissection table where she did the bulk of her carving, hung a clipboard with a yellow notepad. A large corner of the clipboard had broken off long ago. Knotted to the metal spring hinge of the board was a foot-long frayed piece of brown twine with a carpenter's pencil tied to the end. The back end of the pencil was wrapped four or five times with a piece of white cloth tape that had turned dark pink and served to keep the knotted twine from sliding off the pencil. A large eraser hung from a second piece of string tied to the other end of the hinge. It had never been used. She preferred the flat, rectangular carpentry pencil over the standard style mainly because it was easier to sharpen (using any handy knife from her vast collection). Plus, it had a familiar feel when she used it, like that of a scalpel.

Since Mr. Doe was in no hurry to leave, Dr. Montez interrupted her cutlery work to demonstrate her 'trick'. She placed the sectioned liver aside in an eight by ten inch tray and placed it next to the body. Using the knife, she dipped the tip of the blade deep in the hollowed chest cavity of the patient where the darkest blood had pooled and lifted it out, lightly tapping the blade on Mr. Doe's ribcage to knock off excess blood. Reaching to the clipboard she made three quick strokes to form the letter "R" She had to quickly flip the blade over to have just enough blood to finish the tail of the letter. Dipping again, she made two straight lines joined at the corner to form an "L". "You see?" she asked. She did it once more, but this time narrating, "One, two, *tree* lines— that make 'R'; One, *two* lines—that make 'L'. Right lung have *tree* lobes; Left lung have *two*. Easy! See? You not forget, right?"

Later that same year, when I had to sweat out my first college anatomy & physiology exam, I knew I'd get the one right about the lobes of the lungs.

*   *   *

The ability to remember the minutia of anatomy & physiology, as well as other classes was an important skill. One I would come to depend on daily. Performing CPR, for example, would fall into the same category. Not only performing CPR, simply *getting* to the cardiac arrest scene in the shortest possible time was of paramount importance. The Metropolitan Medical Center (where years later I returned to work as a Respiratory Therapist) was an enormous campus and it was essential to be able to first locate, then recall the shortcuts to all critical care areas.

One such route actually linked the Surgical ICU with the Medical ICU, a path frequently traveled by staff. Although technically a restricted area, the trail served as a direct link from one unit to the other, saving at least five minutes of walking. The only problem was that it was through the core of the maternity ward and passed the mothers' designated breast feeding area.

The nurses would get testy when they saw us coming but the benefit of saving precious minutes along with an occasional bonus glimpse of a bare, swollen breast made the shortcut well worth the dirty looks.

*   *   *

Codes were inevitable at the Met, and frequent. When I worked the day shift as an RT, it seemed like you could count on one being called every couple of shifts.

Each hospital has its own language of communication to alert staff in various emergencies. Be it a cardiac arrest, suspected fire, lost or wandering patient, or a baby abducted from maternity, each crisis has a specific number (or phrase) that is announced and radioed via pagers to a select team of responders.

Late one morning at Metropolitan, we had completed our first two sets of treatments and ventilator rounds with nothing unusual to report. It had been fairly quiet. For that reason we knew to expect the worst before the end of our shift. It wasn't long before we heard the adrenalin-pumping phrase overhead: *"CODE 7—WEST ENTRANCE—CITY BUS."*

Fortunately, it was not my day to carry the code beeper. Unfortunately for Lou, one of my fellow therapists, the beeper went off in his coat pocket while seated in the men's room stall. He managed to consolidate his efforts, did his best Clark Kent, and burst out of the restroom, running toward the main entrance and bracing himself for the nineteen-degree January air.

The problem wasn't that a city bus was carrying a cardiac arrest victim. The problem was that the bus stop was on the south-bound side of the street with no less than six lanes of traffic separating it from the front door where Lou and the other team members stood shivering and panting.

Nicole Blake, a short red-haired nurse from the ER we called 'Nic' was the first to respond to the page. She was an aggressive little maverick that surprisingly turned out to be a great leader. She grabbed the stretcher from her department on the way out, and headed through the ambulance doors along the side of the building to join the others. "Let's go *now!*" she screamed as she took off across the street against the flashing 'Do Not Walk' sign.

Standing a hair above five feet, she was forced to bend at the waist far enough to build the momentum needed to move the hundred pound stretcher up the street grade and across the lanes of traffic. This served to hide her from view for anyone ahead of her. To passing motorists, it gave the appearance of an empty stretcher gliding through traffic.

Nicole used her stature to her advantage anyway. Should an on-coming car fail to stop, the stretcher would be the first casualty, except for the fact that it was mounted with a fully pressurized oxygen cylinder which, if struck, would generate an explosion the likes of which would mimic a small bomb.

*   *   *

The victim was the driver of the bus. He was a rotund man in his sixties who'd spent most of his time sitting behind the wheel eating hamburgers and fries. Slumped, unconscious and draped in yellow fast food wrappers, the embroidered patch on his uniform shirt simply read "Clarence".

Since people didn't have the convenience (or annoyance) of cell phones back then, one of the passengers recognized the trouble and took the initiative to run up the aisle, lift the radio microphone off its hook, and make an awkward distress call to the dispatcher. Something along the lines of: "Uh... may day... may day. We got us an emergency here. Ya'll better hurry-up too... old Clarence here's 'bout to croak!"

The dispatcher, in turn, wisely contacted hospital staff as well as the nearest police station, which happened to be the recently revived MPU—(Mounted Patrol Unit). Although horses had not been used for nearly a century, a group of ten had been reintroduced in 1971 in order to help patrol the extensive grounds of Forest Park.

The team followed Nic across the lanes of traffic, taking wide strides in a single line. To the stopped drivers, it must have looked like the cover of the Beatles' *Abbey Road* album, except that everyone was dressed in white.

By this time almost three minutes had passed since the announcement of the code and unless CPR was initiated soon, they would reach that awful point of no return— irreversible brain damage for Clarence.

In the brisk January air, Nicole's face blushed as red as her hair as she got to the front of the bus. Out of breath and dripping snot on the white stretcher sheet, she maneuvered it so that the edge of the mattress rested against the front bumper of the bus, keeping it from rolling into traffic.

Since there wasn't time to lift the stretcher over the curb and drag it through the frozen grass to the folding bus door, this would have to do. The police had not arrived and the cars kept coming, the drivers rubber-necking their way past the scene.

While Nicole secured the stretcher, three other team members jumped up the two deep metal steps leading into the cabin and began a quick assessment of the victim.

No pulse, no respirations, but pupils still responded... barely. It was obvious they needed to get him to the stretcher so CPR could be started. Lou was one of the three who strained to lower the fat man to the floor as quickly as possible and slide him through the doorway feet first.

Two rescuers struggled to support Clarence's enormous mid-section and head while freeing him from his seat, Nicole waited below, ready to catch his feet and legs.

Clarence's face had taken on a grayish-purple shade with his swollen tongue sticking halfway out between thick, dry lips. As they tried to move in unison with their backs hunched, the team started waddling toward the door of the bus like a nervous group of shuffling penguins.

Once pulled free of the doorway, it was only a short drag from the bottom step to the edge of the curb where the lowered stretcher was waiting. At this point, Lou had already begun tilting the head back so he could ventilate Clarence with a bag-mask.

Dr. Kinley, one of the team members and resident MIC (manager in charge) at the scene, screamed for someone to start chest compressions. He didn't want to delay another second, but the straps were still being fastened around the patient—and the stretcher hadn't yet been raised to the upright and locked position for transport across the street.

Responding in typical fashion, Nic wasted no time securing the legs and feet, and lunged forward—landing on the hips of Clarence as she straddled him. Tucking her feet under his legs for stability, she began chest compressions, pausing only briefly for ventilations from Lou. She was positioned just inches from the grill of the bus and could feel the heat coming off the engine block. Although this helped warm her hands, she was becoming nauseated from the oil and exhaust fumes that lingered in the cold air.

The other team members had gathered at the far edge of the stretcher and managed to swing the side nearest the bus away from the bumper, so it could be raised to the rolling position. Nicole and Lou kept the rhythm... *One thousand one - one thousand two - one thousand three - one thousand four - one thousand five—breathe!*

Small pieces of broken curb and shards of amber-colored Seagram's bottles were quickly kicked aside. Bending over to grip the freezing metal handles, the team counted to three, released a chorus of groans as Nic, the nearly-dead driver, and the stretcher were all elevated and ready to roll.

As the stretcher was positioned, the unmistakable rhythmic clop of horse hooves was heard. The cavalry had arrived! The three MPU officers had come to lead the return across the street. Two of the Mounted Patrol Officers had already positioned themselves to block traffic in each direction, while the third shouted instructions for the team to follow, directly behind his magnificent horse, Buddy, who looked big as a Clydesdale.

Once the momentum started, they began their trek across the street toward the ER entrance—while dozens of onlookers sat behind their wheels in silent disbelief... *one thousand one - one thousand two - one thousand three...*

They had nearly reached the halfway point when Buddy unexpectedly slowed, reducing the gap between his back hooves and the stretcher's front wheels. The code team barely noticed as they concentrated on steering the wobbly stretcher over bits of gravel and patches of ice. The important task now was to safely push the stretcher in a straight line, keeping everything moving forward without losing either passenger.

* * *

A sixty-nine year old man named Ed Timmons sat in his car at the head of the three blocked lanes, awaiting the passing of this strange parade. Timmons was on his way to see his wife who was recovering from surgery the day before.

He was in the north-bound far right lane, waiting to pull into the Metropolitan parking garage. The second MPU officer, who was holding back traffic, was about fifteen feet in front of Timmons' car and a few feet to his left. As Timmons explained to the Surgical ICU nurses later that morning, this created a perfect vantage point.

According to the MPU officer who rode Buddy, it is not uncommon for a newly-introduced horse to become exceptionally stubborn or moody from time to time. Some literally get depressed if they are under stress for any length of time. The horse's superior level of intelligence combined with distinct personality traits can cause unusual behaviors.

But that wasn't Buddy's problem.

The horses had been purchased, ten in all, from one of the top rural breeders in eastern Kentucky. Once the foals had matured, they were transported from the grassland farm to the Forest Park stables in St. Louis. The new, comparatively plush accommodations, for some reason, disagreed with Buddy. What also disagreed with him was his change in feed—from the broad selection of rich grass pastures—to bucket upon bucket of specially formulated grain and soy-based meal. This soon resulted in what was later diagnosed as severe gastritis. Buddy had developed an enormous stomach ache.

"Scouring" is a term used in equine circles to describe the rapid and massive fluid loss associated with the condition, and is often accompanied by a risk of death. In other words... Buddy was about to have explosive diarrhea. And, according to trainers and breeders who have experienced the unsightly event, the word "scour" fits perfectly. First, the horse's intestines are scoured. Then, all within squirting distance soon require a thorough scouring of their own... skin, teeth, clothing, shoes, and anything else within range.

*　*　*

Timmons recounted the scene to his wife and her nurse minutes after it happened. He said he'd never, in his nearly seventy years, seen anything quite like it. Buddy had stopped directly in front of Timmons' car, as if startled. He slowly raised his head, snorted a long puff of steam out of his nostrils and lifted his tail, signaling the onslaught.

Expecting the familiar cylinder-shaped clumps that form manure piles he'd seen at the zoo and farms—Timmons was not prepared for the rich, steamy blast of mud that exploded out of Buddy's butt and down his hind-quarters. Like bubbling crude, Buddy had let loose with the fury and majesty of Yellowstone's Old Faithful... only sideways.

The team was able to slow the stretcher to a rolling stop once they'd seen the tail go up. It wasn't the first time. Horses dump in the street all the time, wherever they please. At most, they'd have to watch their step once Buddy finished, making sure none of the wheels ran through the pile. Nicole had interrupted her count when she saw Buddy's tail and realized the thunderous river coming out was not what it was supposed to be. *One thousand four - one thousand five... Shiiiit!*

Unfamiliar with the term 'scour,' Ed described what he saw as "one big brown Niagara." Once the flow had stopped, two loud pops of gas followed. The pops were what did the most damage. Clusters of grape-size bullets peppered the team.

Timmons expressed amazement at the fact that once the team had been hit, they never missed a beat. They just squinted, wiped their faces on their sleeves, and trudged on—looking like Dalmatians but determined to get inside. Nic, of course, had borne the brunt of the nasty spatter since she was perched higher than the others; eye-to-*eye*, so to speak. She later admitted that in a strange way—for a split second at least—the 'shower' had helped warm her.

After Buddy's dramatic debut, the procession quickly resumed and the newly decorated parade members made their way past Edward Timmons' front bumper to the curb.

The ER Medical Director, Dr. Spencer Holman, was waiting just inside the automatic doors watching in disbelief and shaking his head. Holman could be an abrasive, pompous ass a good part of the time. But having seen him in action, there is no one I'd rather have work on me if I was the one on the stretcher.

Never one to miss an opportunity to dish an insult, Holman watched as the team steered past him, heading for

Trauma Room 2. Seeing the brown, encrusted face of Nicole pass by as she breathlessly pumped on the chest of Clarence, Holman said, "Nic, you not only looked like a bull rider out there—you smell like one."

Staring at him and dripping brown sweat, she squinted and replied, "Don't push your luck, Holman. That could have been you out there surfing that brown wave."

*   *   *

At the end of the shift, Nicole summed up her feelings about how she viewed her job as a special kind of calling. She spoke of Dr. Holman's condescending attitude and the wacky events of the day, as well as the emotional toll on a person who chooses to work in a hospital.

"Considering the politics in this place, and what we just went through to get that patient inside this building," she offered. "It's really just another day at the Met."

"Same problem, different asshole."

—Chapter 5—

First, do no Harm

"If I have done amiss, impute it not!
The best may err"

Joseph Addison
Cato: A Tragedy Act V, scene 4

GREGORY R. FROST, RRT

Although the Hippocratic Oath is most often associated with graduating medical school students, its guiding principle in caring for the sick and injured is paramount—*First, do no harm.* The foundation upon which all assessment, decisions, and performance of duties associated with such a challenging endeavor must be built on compassion. Nothing less. Without it healthcare is futile.

Assume for the moment that care delivered to hospitalized patients is based upon the premise of sacrificial service and a desire to see the person become disease-free, or at the very least more healthy at discharge compared with the condition at the time of admission.

Despite the universal goal, mishaps are as certain as the sunrise. Looking at it from a global perspective—devastating mistakes are no doubt made every single day. Whether they involve the wrong leg, the wrong lung, the wrong breast, or the wrong patient altogether, human nature hails its own weakness and vulnerability.

At any given moment, somewhere, someplace, odds are a healthcare professional is about to make a terrible decision.

* * *

One of the most troubling incidents occurred during my final year as a staff therapist at Metropolitan. It was a banner year for the bizarre, including the man who walked into the emergency room late one evening carrying an old canister-style Hoover vacuum. We assumed he was a salesman. It may have seemed a bit strange to watch him walk so quickly toward the ER to make his pitch, but quickly understandable when you followed the trail of the hose. From the front of the vacuum, the hose drooped down and brushed along the floor before looping upward, disappearing inside the man's unzipped pants. A hard problem for sure.

Another frequent patron of the emergency room was a young man who had a fondness for sharp objects. Every month or so, a young man I'll call Roger would come in complaining of severe abdominal cramps. Every x-ray revealed the same thing—foreign body ingestion, or *FBI*. Usually, the item was determined to be small enough to pass on its own. Occasionally, though, an intervention was required by the on-call gastrointestinal specialist. With the help of his trusty four-foot flexible endoscope, the removal would be skillfully accomplished and Roger sent home. What made his last visit so special was because of what the x-ray revealed. It became the talk of the department for days.

I would not have believed the nurses had I not seen the film myself. *Fifty-two* metallic objects were identified in his stomach, including assorted thumbtacks, nails, needles, push pins, and a small razor knife blade, similar to the one I used in art class. Following extensive surgery, Roger once again recovered and was sent on his way. I left the Met before he had a chance to make an encore appearance. Fifty-two would have been hard to top.

This propensity to self-mutilate is more common and costlier than many realize. An article I came across some years ago documented over 300 medical interventions performed to remove *FBI*'s in thirty-three patients over eight years with a cost to the hospital and taxpayers of more than $2 million. Self-mutilation, then, could be categorized as one of the worst forms of abuse. The intent is clear. Negligence, on the other hand, carries a more broad definition and suggests some kind of personal failure resulting in the unintended injury of another... personal failure that creates a dreadful, sick feeling within the offending caregiver.

I know this feeling.

When my firstborn, Kevin, developed allergies at the age of three, the testing showed severe reaction to multiple triggers, so a regimen of weekly injections under the direction of a pediatric allergist was required. Of the more than 70 needle scratches made on his back during the screening, nearly all were hot spots.

When the doctor came into the exam room to share his findings, the first words out of his mouth were, "This kid's allergic to *everything*." He needed weekly injections and they could be done either in the doctor's office or at home. We opted for home.

* * *

The lines etched on the side of the tiny syringe indicating the dose were confusing from the start. Besides, it didn't look like the same kind of syringe used at the doctor's office. That presented the first problem.

The second was that I didn't want to give Kevin the shots. He never really complained, but I knew he hated it. So I often had a tendency to rush the job, hoping to minimize his anxiety and mine. As expected, on one of the early attempts I had misread the prescription and moved the decimal point. I essentially gave Kevin a hefty overdose.

Fortunately, when the adverse reaction symptoms began (within a minute) we realized my mistake and drove to the nearest ER for a shot of epinephrine.

But the mishap that happened one day in the ER at Metropolitan was so troubling, it's impossible for me to forget.

It was my turn to carry the code pager. When the night therapist handed it over he shook his head saying, "Good luck man. The medics just radioed. They're bringing in a forty-five year old with burns all over—one of the worst. Don't be surprised when you get the call."

The ambulance ETA was about eighteen minutes. Not enough time for a quick run to the cafeteria for breakfast or coffee for that matter. No time to start reviewing last night's shift report and treatment schedule for the day. No time for anything... but to wait.

One of the hardest parts of a caregiver's role may very well be inactivity. The waiting can be tough. Our job, after all, is to *do something* for the patient; to be proactive and use the knowledge gained to solve the problem at hand. Same is true for the families. Waiting can be agonizing since they're fed so little information, yet at the same time instructed to relax.

I didn't have to wait long before the pager went off.

* * *

The Met held the designation of a Level I Trauma Center, but not as a Burn Center. The hospital was never designed, nor was it equipped, to handle severely burned patients. Those were almost always air-lifted to a county facility for special treatment and expertise not available at the Met. So, about sixteen minutes after the night therapist handed me the pager as I trotted into Trauma Room 1, the idea of our inability to handle burn patients was all I could think about. Why were they bringing him here? Maybe he lived so close to the Met that they couldn't risk transport time to a burn unit.

Then I saw him. Sonny. Our burn victim, who we soon discovered had not been *anywhere* near a flame. Not even a cigarette.

At the moment I jogged into the room, he was being slid onto the treatment table by a mass of gloved hands. The condition of the naked, bloated body was repulsive. I couldn't tell if he was black, white, or bi-racial. His skin was split open over every area of his body. It was if he had been drug across a bed of nails face down, then flipped over and drug again to even things out.

The deeply split skin wounds were curled at the edges like cabbage leaves, and the raw pink flesh shined under the glare of the lights. The skin was literally sloughing off—right before our eyes.

Sonny was melting.

Accompanying the rapid skin slough was an awful smell of pus, raw tissue, and decomposition. I couldn't begin to imagine what was happening on the *inside* of his body let alone the outside.

Since my department was located next to the ER, I was one of the first to arrive. There were two staff members already at work on Sonny, a physician and an RN. They had gotten past the shock of his appearance and started CPR.

Their technique was dreadfully ineffective, not because of skill level, but because the sloughing skin made chest compression and mask ventilation nearly impossible. The physician on duty, Dr. Cohn, struggled to keep his interlocked fingers centered on the lower half of the sternum while the wet, slimy tissues presented a dangerously slippery surface.

The nurse was just as frustrated trying to create and maintain a tight seal over Sonny's face with the bag-mask resuscitator. Bits of skin around his nose and chin loosened and began folding over around the cushion of the triangle-shaped mask. Without a good seal, effective ventilation was out of the question. Until the anesthetist showed up to insert the airway tube—it was either a mask or mouth-to-mouth. The nurse wisely continued bagging.

At that point the three of us were still the only ones in the room working on Sonny. The code summons was repeated, and my pager sounded again. I was moving over to relieve the nurse when Dr. Cohn huffed out orders between compressions, saying that he needed to start a central line to get fluids in. Looking at me, he jerked his head toward the patient and said, "Take over."

With no time to stretch on a pair of gloves, I shouldered myself next to him to keep the rhythm, and readied my hands by interlocking the fingers. I stood at Sonny's side just above his chest and quickly placed my palms on the lower sternum as Dr. Cohn removed his. This was the early 70's, before the Centers for Disease Control had mandated the Universal Precautions protocol. This meant gloves were optional.

The flesh was warm, brittle, and runny, and his matted chest hair was coarsely sticky. The putrid smell wafting up wasn't unlike maggoty meat and was strong enough to make me wish I had worn a mask.

As we switched off, the doctor quickly grabbed an intravenous line to start, while I struggled to keep my hands in place during each compression. The tissues were weeping so badly that I was forced to swipe a towel on the area after every few sets of compressions. At one point, my hands slid off-center and I felt (and heard) the unmistakable crack of a rib.

To help illustrate how difficult it was to perform CPR on Sonny, if you would cut, say, a two-foot square section of a kid's Slip N' Slide toy, drenched it in oil, shredded it with a knife, and *then* placed it on Sonny's chest—you might come close to duplicating the conditions.

At last, another resident was able to break away from treating an acute asthmatic teen down the hall and came to take over. I gladly backed away. But before I could relieve the nurse who was bagging Sonny, I had to wipe Sonny's sloughed skin from my hands. For an instant, before grabbing the towel, I looked down at my palms and shuddered. I felt like Pontius Pilate—riddled with guilt over the whole affair. The skin, the stench, the cracked ribs... this had to be the most disastrous code ever.

I wiped the slime off as best I could and tossed the soiled towel between Sonny's legs. No sense throwing it on the floor and slipping on it. I positioned myself at the head of the stretcher. The nurse held the bag-valve mask in place while I clawed the fingers of my left hand around the mask and slimy jaw. I began breathing for Sonny.

There, as I hovered behind Sonny's head and above his face, it occurred to me that this was the *same* image captured on the college brochure years earlier. The details, though, were distinctly different—*her* hands weren't covered in rotted tissue and *she* didn't appear to be on the verge of vomiting. Repulsed, frustrated, and angry that anesthesia hadn't shown up, I blurted out, "Why didn't they take this guy to the closest Burn Unit?"

Dr. Cohn never looked up from securing the central line he had just inserted and said in a strangely calm voice, "That's because this is *not* a burn patient. This is a drug reaction. The man is in anaphylactic shock, and if you can't do a better job ventilating him Mr. Therapist, we might as well quit now." Like a dog caught peeing on the carpet I wanted to crawl away.

The anesthetist on call finally graced the scene with his presence, chewing a large mouthful of breakfast. He seemed annoyed at being paged twice. Pulling the curtain aside and sauntering into the room, he was just in time to hear my lecture from Dr. Cohn. Probably made his day.

With the tube placed between Sonny's vocal cords and a quick listen with a stethoscope—the anesthetist nodded and was out of the room in less than two minutes, still chewing.

*   *   *

Sonny was dead by mid-morning. No cocktail of drugs could counter what had been set in motion. I was as disappointed in my performance and troubled by the fact I had to observe Sonny's very last breath—which I had given. The code was officially called. Time of death: 8:39 a.m.

Not long after his wife arrived and was given the news, other information surfaced offering a much clearer picture of what actually had happened to Sonny. We learned his real name was "Sun" (pronounced 'soon'). His mother was from Korea. She had married an American soldier who was serving in Seoul, the two later emigrating to the U.S. as husband and wife. Sun's father had never liked the name for his boy, so 'Sonny' stuck from birth.

According to his wife, Sonny recently began having seizures, as many as several dozen a day. It made living a normal life difficult and exhausting. A number of medications and treatments were tried. Most failed, producing little relief if any.

So the Harris couple found a neurologist who prescribed a popular broad spectrum medication (carbamazapine), typically used to treat seizure disorders, bi-polar mood swings, and a facial nerve inflammation known as trigeminal neuralgia. What was not well known several years ago was the fact that some people with South Asian ancestry carry a genetic risk factor which can cause severe allergic reactions when carbamazapine is used.

People like Sonny.

The drug has a tendency to reduce the number of blood cells normally produced by the body. When this happens in extreme cases a condition may develop known as "TEN" or *toxic epidermal necrosis.* Once the connection was discovered, the FDA immediately issued an alert warning consumers of the dangers associated with the drug in patients who are genetically predisposed. South Asian Indians appear to have a tenfold risk of reaction and possible death. Today, screening is available (and recommended) for any patient of Asian ancestry prescribed carbamazapine.

From the online *Merck Manual,* a brief description of symptoms:

Within 1 to 3 weeks after the start of the offending drug, patients develop early symptoms of malaise, fever, headache, cough and conjunctivitis. In severe cases of TEN, large sheets of epithelium slide off the entire body at pressure points, exposing weepy, painful, skin. Painful oral crusts, erosions and genital problems accompany skin sloughing in up to 90% of cases. Bronchial epithelium may also slough, causing cough, pneumonia, pulmonary edema, and hypoxemia. Hepatitis may develop.

Skin slippage.

Like a shredded Slip n' Slide.

—Chapter 6—

A Matter of Jurisdiction

"Justice delayed is justice denied"

William E. Gladstone,
Prime Minister of Britain

L ike anything else, medical slip-ups are unavoidable because humans are involved. Even the finest institutions and the most brilliant minds in the land will occasionally suffer a lapse in judgment. The hope is to keep the frequency to a minimum and learn from the mistakes.

More troubling than a simple error in judgment is a philosophy of caring that becomes warped. For example, when describing her work relationship as co-counselor at a crisis center with Ted Bundy, author Ann Rule had no idea that Bundy was a rapist and murderer. Her book, *The Stranger Beside Me,* delves into the mind and motive of a psychopathic serial killer.

There was a stranger working beside me at the Met. His name was Jack Parson.

Jack was in his twenties. Hired near the end of my second year, we discovered that we shared similar interests and developed a friendship. He loved music of all kinds, dabbling with an acoustic guitar in his spare time. Jack was single and lived in a small apartment in the city. Much like Peter at St. Bart's, Jack could handle a guitar and we would occasionally get together to play. I was fairly good at finger-picking, but Jack never seemed to get the hang of it. He would listen to me do a short riff on my Gibson and try his hardest to duplicate it as his fingers cramped. Frustrated, he'd drop his guitar in its case and light up a joint.

Parson had the look of a Haight-Ashbury hippie. Gaunt with full beard and shoulder length hair, his penetrating blue eyes created an intense presence. He was strung tight and vented his frustration in dark, subtle ways. Often silent and moody, he would disappear for hours at a stretch. I wondered what his patients thought as he quietly drifted into the room to give a breathing treatment—saying nothing as he slowly set up the equipment and stared into space.

He initiated profound but disturbing conversations. Between shifts as the group discussed the status of patients, Jack would offer his opinion of ventilator-dependent patients. "Some of these Gomers," he would insist, "have absolutely *no* business being on a vent. It costs a ton of dough, it's a drain on the system, and the people that are *supposed* to care for them don't really care anyway."

The reaction from the group was always the same. Silence. No one wanted to engage in heavy debate with him, especially at 7:00 in the morning. After a couple of rants, I wasn't the only one starting to wonder where he really came from and what RT program he attended. All we could ever get out of him was some place near San Francisco, and that he would be headed back soon. To him, St. Louis was forever a dead town. The guy gave us the willies.

* * *

Morning ventilator rounds were usually assigned to the person who clocked-in first. It became our unofficial reward—once you finished rounds you could stop by the café and dawdle a bit before heading back to the department for the next group of assignments. The rest of the team would be scattered throughout the complex, performing their first set of treatments while you sat mulling over coffee, bagel and cream cheese, and a copy of someone's Globe-Democrat newspaper.

But it could go either way. When it came to vent rounds it was feast or famine. There could be as few as one or two going in the ICU's, which meant you could knock it out in less than thirty minutes. Pull your little supply cart into the unit, change the tubing circuit, fill the humidifier, check the alarms, smile at the family, and away you go.

On the other hand, there could be as many as 14 pumping away at any given time. During flu season, additional units would be rented from a medical supply company or borrowed from neighboring hospitals. Days like that, you did nothing but vents the whole shift.

GREGORY R. FROST, RRT

The model used at the Met was an MA-1 Volume Ventilator, a huge box on wheels the size of a top-loader washing machine. Weighing in at 220 pounds, it was the pride of the Puritan-Bennett company. Developed in 1967, the workhorse unit became the standard in the industry, virtually replacing the iron lung. The ventilator had a control panel consisting of ten dials, multiple alarms, switches, and a pole-mounted bellows-style spirometer which rose and fell inside a clear, graduated cylinder. The bellows, which looked like the pleats on an accordion, opened and closed as it measured the volume of each breath. It was one of the first things you noticed when you walked into a patient's room.

One of the most important components of the MA-1 was the cascade humidifier mounted on the side of the ventilator. With fill-to markings and a built-in heating element, the humidifier produced the warm moist air required by the body. Absent the side markings, this round plastic reservoir could easily pass for a sturdy cereal bowl. The daily practice of monitoring cascade fluid level proved to be key in the death of one of our patients, Florence Mitchell, a tiny frail woman who had been comatose since heart surgery three weeks earlier.

Often the ICU nurses would fill the cascades on their own, before we made rounds. On more than one occasion, I discovered a respiratory-distressed patient with a dangerously low breath volume appearing in the spirometer—only to learn that the patient's nurse had screwed the cascade bowl on crooked, creating a substantial leak.

A potent chemical sterilant (glutaraldehyde) was used to clean the components of the vent between patients. After a few cycles in an industrial washer, the cascade bowl tended to become opaque, preventing accurate readings of fluid levels. The gluteraldehyde was powerful enough to kill anything, even bugs like staphylococcus and streptococcus. And, of course, there was pseudomonas—the infamous gram-negative bacteria that was the RT's nemesis. Seems fitting that the chemistry of the glutaraldehyde formula also lends itself well to other industry uses—like the tanning of leather for example, or processing X-ray film, and, not surprisingly, embalming a corpse.

We were confident that every time we loaded the washing machine with sputum encrusted breathing circuits, mucus-coated mouth-pieces, and slimy face masks—they would come out of the final spin cycle spot-free and clean enough to lick.

It was therefore imperative to keep the cascade's level of distilled water at its maximum in order to provide patients like Florence with an adequate gas/moisture mixture. Pumping hot dry oxygen directly into the airways through an empty bowl could produce disastrous results. In a case like that, the patient might as well be sucking on a blow-torch, and Jack Parson knew exactly how important it was to check the distilled water level on every set of rounds.

*   *   *

One brisk fall morning in November, I was delayed in traffic and forty minutes late for work. Jack Parson happened to be early, the first to report. No surprise, since he was probably up most of the night playing his guitar and smoking bad weed.

It was still dark when Jack pulled into a 'No Parking' zone along the curb several blocks from the hospital. He once told me during one of our Friday night guitar sessions that the long walk to the ER entrance gave him time to mentally and spiritually prepare for the day, particularly after a restless night.

Being the early bird, he was allowed the usual option of taking ventilator rounds, which he often did. Gathering up the check-list sheets and stocking the small stainless steel cart with fresh breathing circuits, extra oxygen set-ups, and several gallon jugs of sealed, distilled water provided by Central Supply, Jack made his way to the elevator and up to the second floor ICU, where the critically ill post-op surgery patients were monitored. Patients like Florence.

The day was expected to be light, with only three vents between the two ICU's. By the time I found a parking spot and walked in at 7:45, Parson would have been on his second cup of coffee with his face buried in the newspaper.

Since I was late, I didn't stop by the café to grab my usual morning cup. Instead, I headed straight to the time-clock downstairs by the department. That's when I bumped into another therapist named Lou, who had been running and was short of breath. "Have you seen Parson?" he huffed in a shaky voice.

"Just got here," I said. "I haven't seen anyone yet. What's going on?"

With a sick look on his face, he said, "Jack just filled Florence's cascade with glutaraldehyde. She'll be dead by noon and he's nowhere to be found!"

Parson had, in fact, vanished—probably traveling that very minute west-bound, in the general direction of California.

Lou was right. Florence had quickly developed a toxic pulmonary foam condition, and her heart failed within a few hours. The frothy, yellow bubbles began backing-up in the air hoses causing the ventilator's pressure alarm to sound repeatedly.

No matter how much she was suctioned, the foam kept coming while the odor from deep in her lungs escaped into the room producing eye-stinging fumes. Even after swapping-out the entire ventilator for a clean unit, the damage had already been done, and Florence was drowning in poison.

After she died, the room had to be sealed off for days before any patient could take the same bed.

PERMISSION TO OBSERVE

The police were immediately contacted (as well as the hospital's attorneys), but Jack Parson had left the building, and our lives.

*   *   *

Standing outside the vacated room made me sick. Not so much from the lingering fumes, but from the thought of a co-worker deliberately violating that precious oath—*First, do no harm.* Even though I desperately wanted to believe that he was just stoned when he loaded that cart, perhaps mistakenly grabbing a chemical jug instead of the distilled water, I couldn't justify it. I couldn't *make* it make sense. I knew him too well. I think he did exactly what he intended. In his eyes, he probably performed a valuable service.

The existence of professional mercy killers has been documented for some time. The behavior of this type of sociopath is unsettling and appalling. Years after working with Parson, I came across a compelling book entitled *Blind Eye,* by James B. Stewart. Written in 1999, Stewart dramatically chronicles the true story of one of the most prolific serial killers in U.S. history—a physician by the name of Michael Swango. His trail of death wove its way through some of the most hallowed halls of healthcare, as well as a remote village in the African Republic of Zimbabwe.

Approximately sixty people died at his hand, with dozens more sickened by Swango's preferred method... poison. This unconscionable behavior places him within the ranks of notables like Ted Bundy, Phillip Wayne Gacy, and Donald Harvey, the Ohio nurse aide who confessed to no less than fifty-two murders.

Writer Sir Arthur Conan Doyle (himself a physician), used the voice of Sherlock Holmes to declare: "When a doctor does go wrong he is the first of criminals. He has nerve and he has knowledge."

In the summary at the end of *Blind Eye,* we are provided with some insight into the motives of people like Swango and Jack Parson:

"A psychopath is generally understood to be someone who lacks a capacity for empathy and may exhibit aggressive, perverted, criminal, or amoral behavior. The psychopath tends to be highly self-absorbed. The condition is usually classified as an extreme and dangerous variation of narcissistic personality disorder, narcissism being the excessive love of self. But it is not a form of insanity; psychopaths are fully aware of their actions and of the actions' consequences, and can distinguish right from wrong."

Having spent years in all types of critical care situations, participated in dozens of cardiac arrests, and cared for countless ventilator patients at the brink of death—to suggest that I never once entertained the thought of pulling the plug would be the ultimate deception. Our very makeup as human beings provides ample opportunity to make choices which cover the full range of good, questionable, and horrific acts. Joseph Conrad once wrote, "...a belief in a supernatural source of evil is not necessary; men alone are quite capable of every wickedness."

The Hippocratic Oath, recited by all who begin their professional lives of service and sacrifice, ends with a dual message—that of a blessing and a curse:

"While I continue to keep this Oath unviolated, may it be granted to me to enjoy life and the practice of the art, respected by all men in all times! But should I trespass and violate this Oath, may the reverse be my lot!"

Chapter 7

The Dummy Salesman

"The first law in advertising is to avoid the concrete promise...
And cultivate the delightfully vague"

Phillip Crosby,
New York Herald Tribune, 1947

GREGORY R. FROST, RRT

Although it all started when I saw the brochure in high school, making a difference wasn't always the motive. Big money became another. My young family was growing along with the bills. And besides, I admired the salesmen who would casually stride through the hospital in their shiny wing tip shoes, genuine leather demo bags, and generous expense accounts.

They would gather in the Purchasing Department and talk shop while awaiting a chance to show the latest miracle product to the hospital buyers. They would discuss things like which device company hosted the best sales meeting location, invariably some exotic place in the Caribbean I'd never heard of.

These guys had to be winners, I thought. Why couldn't I do that? How hard could it be? Lord knows, the job as a therapist wasn't exactly a walk in the park. And with my strong clinical background, I could surely get something in the medical device or pharmaceutical industry. The problem was that deep down, I really didn't believe in myself. I couldn't persuade someone to buy something if my life depended on it. I had a fear of public speaking. Paralyzing fear.

I remember sitting at my desk in Mr. Johnson's fifth grade classroom at Fairview Elementary in north St. Louis, filled with dread whenever he asked questions. I'd know when it was coming so I planned accordingly. When he'd wrap up the lesson, he would invariably say, "Now... time for me to ask *you* geniuses some questions."

At that moment, I would re-shape my posture to match that of Miller, the kid who sat directly in front of me. Fortunately, his head was large and I could blend into his outline, becoming virtually invisible to Mr. Johnson.

Each time the question came I would sit dead-still, praying he'd target anyone but me. Staring at Miller's neck just inches away, I noticed he had a string of moles that bore a striking resemblance to the big dipper. I would begin counting the little ones in the handle part of the pattern, lost in thought when I would suddenly hear an explosive, "Frost!"

All four legs of my desk hopped when I realized I'd just been shot by the enemy. "Who's buried in Grant's tomb?" he'd ask. Each of us got *the question* at some point during the year. Funny thing is, he never told us the answer. Not all year. We always thought it was a trick question. Even if one of us made a wild guess and got the darn thing right, all he would do is pause, shake his head and go on to the next victim.

Whenever he called on me, my forehead heated up, my breathing stopped (along with my heart temporarily), I would try to compose myself enough to softly mumble, "I don't know Mr. Johnson."

Then the pause, the head shake, and more questions.

I hated fifth grade.

* * *

Even as a young adult, I trembled at the thought of speaking out. I had married my high school sweetheart at seventeen and we began attending the church where I grew up. It only took being involved in one or two activities like helping teach Sunday school, or playing on the church volleyball team that automatically set you up as a viable target for leading in prayer.

Southern Baptists loved to pray, almost as much as they loved to eat. They prayed about everything; the start of the service, the end of the service, the singing, preaching, eating, playing volleyball... even counting the money... *everything* was preceded by prayer—and therefore had to be led by someone. Like it or not (and I didn't), that's the way it was. Not that I wasn't a firm believer in the benefits of prayer—it was just the public aspect that made me freeze.

At the end of the Sunday morning service, the preacher would quickly scan the pews in hope of making eye contact with someone—anyone—in the congregation to voice the closing prayer and benediction. I always admired those seasoned Deacons who could spontaneously rattle off lofty petitions covering everything that needed to be covered for the day, the week, the year, and, the rest of our lives in less than thirty seconds. That way, we'd have the best chance of beating the Methodists to the lunch buffet. Baptists like fellowship, and they like to eat.

I also figured out when the preacher stood up for the final dismissal, I could bow my head long before anyone else, gripping the pew in front of me so as to strike an intense, worshipful pose (which no one dared interrupt) therefore avoiding a situation like Mr. Johnson's fifth grade class. I would walk away unscathed, sort of like hiding behind the mole-spotted neck, but being spiritual about it of course.

God didn't find my strategy very amusing. It all came crashing down one Sunday at 11:59 a.m. With one minute to go (Baptists *always* let out on time), I was scrunched down in my holy pose focused on counting the belt loops on the obese guy in front of me when I heard, "And now I'm going to ask **GREG FROST** to lead us in our closing prayer."

Like the switch of a time machine, I was immediately transported back to Mr. Johnson's class room. This, along with losing my grip on the pew ahead of me, caused a jolt that must have been obvious to the brethren around me. Had I been Pentecostal, it would have looked like I was either slain by the Holy Ghost or goosed by the guy behind me.

Why me God? You *know* I can't do this. Where do I start? How do I end? When my words finally made their way out, it sounded more like Pig-Latin than a heart-wrenching, blood-sweating prayer. I'm sure it lasted no more than fifteen or twenty seconds and only covered one or two things that I recall. Somehow I managed to get in a swift *"in Jesus' name, Amen.*" and turned to get to the doors for some fresh air.

By the time I made my way to the exit where the preacher shook hands with everyone, sweat began to roll down my temples and soaked the collar of my white shirt. Feeling light-headed and a little nauseous, I inched along with the crowd finally reaching him and shook a warm, dry hand. I started to say, "I'm really sorr—"

But he cut me off by saying, "Fine job Greg. God bless you."

I walked out confused by what he'd just said. I was certain I had just botched my first-ever public prayer. My fear may have been needlessly exaggerated, nonetheless it was real... and persistent.

With such intense anxiety you would expect that I would steer clear of any future role requiring public speaking skills. But I surprised myself by applying for my first sales job.

The interview was for a Territory Sales representative with a company called Anderson Medical Supply, one of the largest distributors of CPR training manikins and educational products in the country. The sales manager was of Swedish descent and bore an uncanny resemblance to actor John Candy. He was an imposing figure named Oscar Swenson who easily tipped the scales at 280 pounds. He used to describe his appearance as that of an ex-football player gone to seed. If hired, I would be reporting directly to him.

He described the role as a cake walk. "It's a pretty easy job," he said. "You just put a few pieces of product literature and catalog in one of these custom logo 3-ring binders, slip your card inside, and hand them out in the hospitals. The numbers will come," he assured me. "A monkey could do it," he added.

"Now I can see," he continued, "that you are *way* over-qualified for the job. And you probably won't take it since I can only start you at $18,000." He paused to let that sink in (Oscar was a master manipulator). "Oh you'll get quarterly bonuses of course... but they'll be based on sales *less* your expenses. So what do you think?"

Sales *less* my expenses? That meant I would use *my* car, *my* gas, *my* insurance, *my* credit card, with everything being subtracted from my sales each quarter. If anything was left... that was my bonus. Basically, I'd be paying my own way.

Assuming I was a strong negotiator, at this point, I would highlight the value I bring to the organization as a qualified, experienced RT clinician. I would also emphasize the fact that I already possess a firm grasp and understanding of the products I would be selling. And by doing so, I could hold out for a higher base salary and get a much more attractive offer.

"I'll take it," I said.

That was on a Thursday afternoon. Not missing a beat Oscar replied, "Here's the catch. I need you in Chicago for a week of sales training—starting Monday."

The company had always been family owned, and every decision was made by the founder, Walter (The Old Man) Anderson, an unlikely salesman who started the business in his garage. From the stained, scuffed wooden floors of the company's original warehouse location in Chicago, to the palatial offices of their new suburban locale, things changed rapidly.

When the sales force was flown in for the grand opening and tour of the new corporate office, it became clear who would be footing the bill for the new headquarters which included a private lake, a softly burning fireplace behind The Old Man's solid mahogany desk, and the 100% cotton monogrammed towels—untouched and neatly draped on a gold bar in a private bathroom adjacent his office.

Like a butcher at a deli case weighing the meat, The Old Man's finger was often on the scale - but I was successful anyway and thoroughly enjoyed my work for several years. The freedom of the job was what appealed to me most. My office was in my home, 300 miles from the nearest manager. I could schedule (or not) my days as I saw fit.

We were required to provide hand-written call reports each Friday, which The Old Man read with great enthusiasm every Monday at 4:00 a.m. He became even more excited when he noticed something in the call reports he didn't like... such as not enough sales calls in a day, or calls in the wrong departments, not enough travel, or a myriad of other things that infuriated him. These little discoveries often prompted a phone call to let you know exactly how things should be done... his way.

So nearly four decades after the launch of The Old Man's garage business, there we stood. The Anderson Medical sales force. In the plush offices of our fearless leader. Having received our marching orders to increase sales immediately, we wrapped up our tour and scrambled for our belongings in preparation for the ride to O'Hare.

There was a feeling that there was still some unfinished business. Oscar, in typical take-charge fashion, orchestrated the airport departure so each representative knew who to ride with. "Eckstein, you and Davis will ride with Smith. Mitchell, tag along with Kinsey. Frost, you're with me," he said.

As we walked out of the training room, he paused and delivered one last announcement, "Oh, by the way, I didn't want you guys to leave without some good news. The Old Man has generously opted to *increase* your mileage reimbursement... by two cents a mile."

"And," he went on, "Your commission structure has been *modified*. Instead of 12%, starting Monday it will be 8%. Everybody have a safe trip back. Go get 'em!"

On the way to the airport the two California reps, Hampton and Stevens, sat silently in the back while I rode in front with Oscar who was the first to speak.

"Well," he said, "what'd you guys think of the meeting? Good? Was it helpful?" We were all thinking the same thing, but no one said a word. So I did.

"I'll be honest Oscar. I don't think any of us expected to go home with news of a pay cut."

Oscar quickly looked in the rear-view mirror at the others and smiled. Then he turned to me. With a snicker he replied, "Greg my boy, welcome to sales!"

—Chapter 8—

No Explanation Required

"Consider his motives, observe his pleasures.
A man simply cannot conceal himself"

Confucius

GREGORY R. FROST, RRT

One of the benefits of working for a company like Anderson Medical was the endless supply of practical joke props. Along with the staple product line of full-body and torso CPR training manikins, the company was also known for its broad selection of trauma-related manikins and simulators. Hospitals which successfully met the stringent requirements of the Joint Commission on Accreditation of Hospitals (JCAHO) would at some point have practiced disaster drills. These were mock events designed to sharpen the skills of the caregivers and were usually carried out in the emergency room area.

Employees of the hospital would be in full make-up to represent victims injured in some unexpected local disaster like a building collapse, highway crash, or terrorist attack. Various products from Anderson Medical were often purchased to be used in the drill, ranging from fake arms with multiple gashes and exposed bone, to severed limbs or flexible fingers molded from actual human hands.

These were so real that some actually appeared to have badly trimmed nails. On a few models, you'd be able to see scar patterns interrupting the fingerprints. These were splendid for discreetly inserting into someone's third or fourth drink at a party. Better yet, slipping one into the coat pocket of a departing guest would get laughs for quite some time.

The Old Man came up with all the clever names for the manikins. We had the Heimlich maneuver torso called, "Choking Chuckie," which came equipped with a hunk of simulated steak that exploded from a gaping mouth when you squeezed the mid-section. During sales meetings, we'd have contests shooting the plugs across the boardroom table to see who could hit the other's coffee cup.

Or there were the famous "Adam & Eve" models which allowed prostate and pelvic examinations. Adam came with four glands of varying size and texture, while Eve could be penetrated at will.

At a time of rapid company growth, when we seemed to pick up new products almost weekly, we got wind in the field of one particular sample that showed up at headquarters. Every product for catalog consideration went through a rigorous testing protocol personally handled by the company's sole Product Manager, Claudia, a buxom young dark-haired Italian with a heavy accent and little to no medical knowledge. She often found herself serving at the pleasure of The Old Man, accompanying him on flights to international trade shows and boring medical meetings, often being on the road together for days or weeks at a time.

The new simulator Claudia was to evaluate was one which had features unlike any other product ever carried by Anderson. The Old Man took great pride in the quality, value, and innovative nature of the products he chose for his sales force to represent and promote. Once the item was approved, you were expected to show it on *every* call. "You can't sell it if you don't show it," he used to say. You never knew when someone might appreciate a demonstration and find the product perfectly matched to their needs.

The idea for the new simulator was a natural—to provide something that addressed the concern of properly educating the public about the risk of sexually transmitted diseases, and how to insure the best possible protection for everyone. Since the 1980's was fraught with concerns over cross-contamination and the risk of becoming infected, the idea of Universal Precautions was quickly gaining support. Timing, it has been said, is everything. So a field trial was in order.

* * *

Unless you've seen it for yourself, you can't fully appreciate the expression on the face of a hospital purchasing agent at the moment a seven-inch flaccid latex penis streaked with bulging veins is pulled out of a sales bag and propped on the desk.

"Rigid Randy" possessed a set of testicles that were flat on one side, creating a sturdy base which balanced the monster in a perfect rainbow curve. Like a wilted stalk of celery, Randy literally 'bowed' before the customer. The sales rep would then begin the demo with a casual; "And here we have the latest in educational products—the *Condom Application Simulator*. Here's how it works."

The rep would then grab a rubber blood pressure-like bulb connected to an eighteen inch tube leading from Randy's two boys, and discreetly hang it over the edge of the buyer's desk.

Once firmly grasped, he would quickly tighten the valve and begin furiously pumping the bulb with one hand as he touted the many features of the product. Slowly rising to the challenge, old winky would literally eye the customer... all... the way... up.

With the other hand (being careful not to interrupt the rhythm of the demo), the rep would reach into the bag and pull out a fresh condom packet. Using teeth to rip the foil open, he would spit out the torn edge and continue his litany of benefits while Randy stood at full attention.

"Now, here's the beauty of this thing," the rep would say, as the customer sat stone still, waiting for the brain to tell the lungs to resume breathing. "Nobody wants to get the clap or the crabs, right? God forbid they come down with something like AIDS. Besides, if you *have* to use a glove why not be as efficient as possible? The last thing you'd want to happen is that you get all primed and ready to go, and you botch the basics of putting the little guy's hat on, see?" Still no response from the customer.

At this point in the presentation, the salesman would pause to admire Randy's frame, standing proudly at attention and fully protected by the condom. Had the demo been performed by a female rep, this would normally be the time when the prospect would have trouble speaking. Possibly the only thing going through the buyer's mind at that moment was what if his secretary was to walk in to ask about the monthly order status? Or if anyone needed coffee, or maybe wanted to chat about what was on TV last night.

When it really got interesting was when the female rep positioned the simulator and would gently wrap her fingers (usually with glossy red nails), around it with her left hand, like a baseball player drumming fingers on the handle of the bat.

At the same time, she would deftly apply the condom with her right hand, rolling it down Randy's length, tight as bratwurst casing. "There," she'd say, "Now he's ready for duty." She continued, "When it's all over, you just open this valve, let him relax to his original position, and you're ready for the next community class." Then the close... "How many do you think you'll need?"

The rep never got a straight answer. As a matter of fact, not a single order was placed during the field test appointments.

The sales reps reported their findings to Claudia, indicating that the buyers seemed uncomfortable at the notion and wouldn't devote a lot of time to the project. Strangely, the few female reps that took the time to show Randy all mentioned the same thing—none of the male buyers they met with would stand up at the conclusion of the meeting as they normally would. The rep would then tuck Randy back into his carrying case, drop him in the sales bag, and off they'd go to the next appointment.

I can see where a buyer might be a little uncomfortable explaining the purchase of the simulator to superiors. My own pride was tested late one Friday afternoon when I received shipment of a full-body training manikin at my home.

I was scheduled to demo the manikin the following week at a local school of nursing, ironically, the Metropolitan Medical Center School of Nursing. The school and board room where I would be showing the dummy was connected to the very halls I once carted specimens, patients, and corpses.

* * *

"Patient Polly" was the name given to a popular (and ridiculously expensive) training manikin from Anderson Medical that provided nursing students with an opportunity to simulate comprehensive care of a bed-ridden patient.

Polly was one sick dummy. Equipped with a tracheostomy opening in her neck, she required complete trach care and suctioning. She also had a colostomy, so wound care and proper bag-changing technique could be practiced. The purchaser also had the option of plugging her colostomy thereby allowing her bowels to become impacted. Through it all, Polly just grinned with her slightly yellowed dentures in a wide-eyed eerie sort of way.

Her stare was ghostly. She had larger than life eyeballs which allowed for ophthalmology care. One prosthetic eye was removable for cleaning and polishing.

Polly reminded me of a TV program I watched as a kid, "The Paul Winchell and Jerry Mahoney Show." One of the characters introduced by Winchell was the aptly-named "Knucklehead Smith." With thick, banana-shaped eyebrows above gaping eyes with no pupils and ears that caught the wind like sails, Knucklehead Smith and Patient Polly could easily have been fraternal twins.

Polly had one other important feature. She could be catheterized and vaginally examined. The urological and obstetrical aspect was not forgotten in the design room. But that wasn't the best part. Polly *also* came equipped with a separate, plastic bag of accessories containing an anatomical device much like that of Randy—an oversized penis equipped with a formidable pair of testicles (this time, whole).

So as a value-added benefit and significant cost savings package, you could alternate between "Polly" and "Perry" with a quick flick of the wrist.

Polly was shipped via truck directly to my home in a six foot wooden box looking very much like Dracula's crate. The driver was a union member and not allowed to lift much more than a finger. As a result, he was unwilling to step beyond the street curb, so I was forced to dig out my two-wheeler buried deep in Christmas clutter before being able to get Polly into the house for inspection.

Standard practice was for the rep to personally deliver the manikin to the prospect for evaluation and pick it up a few days later. This was done for two reasons. The last thing you wanted was for one of the accessories to be missing, or worse, something failing to operate as designed. You wanted to give them ample time to try everything and appreciate all the features.

Second, it was simply cost prohibitive to trust the hospital without a written purchase order. Remember, these are the same people who from time-to-time severed wrong limbs, breasts, and removed the *good* lung. So when a hospital budgets for a $2500 piece of plastic you'd like to be as sure as you can that you've minimized the chance for error.

The opportunity to demo Polly at the Met was my first. I planned to spend the day in my home office, since Oscar had forewarned me about the *don't-you-dare-ask-me-to-lift-this-god-damn-thing* rule of the Teamsters. My youngest son, Nathan (then about the tender, tic-producing age of four) was home with me while Carol picked up some extra hours at work.

"Dad-uh," he'd say (which sounded a lot like the 'plat-uh' in platypus) whenever he saw one of my manikin samples for the first time, "You get lots of cool dolls and stuff." Little did the boy know he was about to meet the grand-daddy of them all.

Once I maneuvered the long pine box into our family room sustaining only one smashed thumb and splinter, I was panting like our golden retriever in August. It didn't occur to me that one of the many selling features of Polly was, in fact, her weight. Although the anatomical features were exaggerated for teaching purposes, she weighed as much as a small adult. This allowed for practice in proper lifting technique and positioning. It also allowed the company the chance to goose up the already astronomical shipping cost to the customer. Finally, it prompted a few colorful words from the sales reps who were told to display Polly at trade show exhibits.

Nate watched anxiously as I grabbed a crow bar and hammer from my tool set to pry off the lid, curious to see what was in Dad-uh's box *this* time. He had seen most of the samples I received, including Choking Chuckie and the CPR dolls. All I really worried about was whether I would have to deal with a shower of foam packing peanuts sticking to my carpet when I pulled her out. Instead, when I lifted the lid, I saw that the entire box was chock-full of straw.

"Where's your doll Dad-uh?" Nathan asked. "Did they forget to put it in the box?"

I was wondering the same thing. So I said, "Let me take a closer look. It has to be in there." Nathan was dressed casually in his t-shirt decorated with several dried Spaghetti-O's, and his slightly yellowed Batman *Underoos*. When it came to appearance, we learned very early that worrying about how he looked was unimportant to him. Nate was one of those kids just as comfortable in straw or dirt, as he was fresh out of the tub.

Not wasting a second as I flipped the lid onto the floor, he dove into one end of the box, standing waist-deep in straw as he began plucking out handfuls left and right, flinging them high in the air.

When I yelled for him to stop the nonsense, I noticed my cheek twitching and jaw clenching. The kid managed to do it every time. I'd have a project that I needed to get done, planned out well in advance and already underway when my little helper would appear... like storm clouds at a picnic.

As he continued to dig, I lifted a large handful of straw from the opposite end of the crate unexpectedly revealing two bulging eyes. The grinning, Knucklehead Smith face was the unmistakable glare of Polly. Prior to that, I had only seen it in the Anderson catalog. I jumped at the sight, immediately tossing the straw back over her face thinking the god-awful stare might just be too much for Nate to handle.

He quickly made his own discovery, spotting a large plastic bag at the bottom of the coffin. The contents of the sack, as expected, proved to be the urology "accessories" which came with the manikin. Inside was a slightly larger-than-life vagina, a 'hoo hoo', as my young grand-daughter called it, along with Perry's generous penis.

At the first sight of the bag next to his feet, Nathan immediately began whooping and hollering like a nervous hyena. Giggling wildly, he grabbed the bag and ripped it open. Barely able to contain himself, he reached inside with a tiny hand and pulled out the fleshy colossus screaming; "Look Dad-uh! A baseball bat shaped like a pee pee!"

With that, he hopped out of the crate and began running laps around the box while wildly swinging the freakish thing overhead like the Lone Ranger. What a wonderful feeling knowing my son takes educational experiences like this so seriously. Another notable trait is that Nathan has always insisted on being first. Call it a competitive edge, but growing up, he always had to be the leader. First in class to get to the playground, first in the neighborhood to get the newest toy, and now—first to answer the front doorbell as he ran into the living room tightly clutching his find.

* * *

I had no idea who it could be. My mind raced at the possibilities while Nate raced through the kitchen. I would have beaten him, had it not been for the fact that I caught the corner of Polly's box with my baby toe on the way.

Stars shot through my head as I limped toward the scene, one that I would never be able to explain. Hopping like a three-legged dog behind the kid, I wondered if it was the mailman, or a salesman. Heaven forbid a deacon from down the street... or the preacher himself!

Worse.

It was Darlene; our twenty-three year old neighbor who had recently been married. Back from her honeymoon, she stopped by to return a pie pan she borrowed from Carol before the trip. Living only a few houses away, she had walked up the hill to return the pan and was greeted by an ecstatic four year-old waving a large penis.

Whenever I think of this story, I have a tendency to recall the things that happened unfolding in slow-motion. Like Nathan, floating toward the door's threshold in an eerie bouncing blur, reaching for the doorknob with his left hand and holding his new treasure in his right—just about the time I round the corner. The little squirt would then stand with his back to me while slowly swinging the "bat" back and forth showing Darlene every detail.

She would be frozen for some time, staring at Perry. Then, in slow motion, her eyes would blink and rise to meet mine. I realized by that time it was useless. Nothing I could say would even be heard by Darlene. She just stared as I limped to the door and opened the latch.

"Hey Dar," I said. "How was the honeymoon?" I saw that her hand holding the pie pan was shaking slightly. My facial tic started again.

"I know this looks kind of weird, but I can explain the whole thing," I said.

"No. That's ok... here," she said, as she slipped the pan through the crack in the door. She turned around heading straight down the hill taking short, quick strides.

Standing at the door wondering why Darlene was leaving so soon, Nathan gripped his new bat and asked, "Didn't she want to play ball Dad-uh?"

All I could say was, "I guess not."

—Chapter 9—

A Real Cut-up

"Aintry?
This-here river don't go nowhere near
Aintry!"

From the film *Deliverance*

PERMISSION TO OBSERVE

O nce I sold my first Patient Polly, subsequent sales of the manikin came more easily. The biggest problem was getting the thing to the hospitals for evaluation. My only option was to prop her up in the front seat of my 1983 Ford Escort Wagon with manual transmission, and take my chances as we passed small clusters of people standing on street corners along the way.

With the less expensive standard transmission, the Escort jerked whenever I shifted gears. In response Polly would unintentionally turn her head in the direction of the onlookers as we lurched from an intersection. As I drove, the vibration from the rough pocked street caused her to slowly return her head to the forward position. Not surprisingly, the observers clutching their paper bag-wrapped bottles would often take a large swig after getting the nod from Polly.

*　　*　　*

After several years (and countless dummy jokes), I began to feel like I had eclipsed my career as a manikin distributor and that I should look for something new. Having sold for Anderson nearly eight years, I was confident making presentations, calling on prospects, and managing my managers. Feeling I had been groomed for something bigger, it was time for a move.

I was surprised one day when I'd gotten an unexpected call from a head hunter about a sales job with a company called Davis & Geck. Described by the recruiter as the second-largest suture manufacturer in the world, I was impressed. Until I found out there were only two. Number one was a company called Ethicon—a powerful division of Johnson & Johnson. They were light years ahead of D & G and enjoyed a commanding market share of 80-90%.

They were especially adept at garnering tenacious surgeon loyalty, due in part to deep pockets containing generous entertainment budgets.

The key customer in this arena wasn't the purchasing agent, nor was it the nurse, or even the hospital CEO. It was the surgeon.

To be successful, a salesman had to make a pitch directly to the end user—the person who called the shots in the bloody trenches of surgery, the one who tied the knots in the suture, and took the glory (or heat) for every stitch. In the early 1990's, that person pulled an awful lot of weight.

A common response to a 30-second D & G sales pitch to the average surgeon during a trot down the hall (if you were fortunate enough to get their attention) would likely produce a response like, *"Don't give me any of that Geck shit, I won't use it. Keep the Ethicon in my room."* The recruiter didn't share that part with me either.

*   *   *

So the opportunity to work in a more disciplined, professional environment intrigued me and set the stage for my typical, thoughtful analysis. "I'll take it," I said.

The recruiter, a country boy with a thick, southern drawl replied, "Whoa there Trigger! You'll need to interview first with the company's Regional Manager, Butch ("Mac") McAllister. Ain't mine to say one way or th'other. Don't even git paid lest the both of you end up sayin' *I do"*. How in the world did this guy get to be a human resource recruiter? Same way I ended up in sales, I guess. God has a sense of humor.

Two weeks later, I met with Mac in his hotel room near the St. Louis airport. He had thin white hair with a thick mid-section. He looked like a white teddy bear with a lot of jewelry. He had three passions. Mac was fond of collecting gold and just as fond of hunting big game in places like Montana and Wyoming. The other thing that drove him was achieving sales goals. Mac expected his seven reps to exceed their quotas regularly. This, of course, allowed him more time to spend on his first two passions. He must have felt that I could further his cause and I soon found myself on a plane to beautiful Newark, New Jersey for training and orientation.

Three grueling weeks later, I completed all required quizzes, written assignments, video-taped role play, and final exam, and I was just getting started. After returning home, Mac called and instructed me to fly to Memphis the following week for field observation with another rep that lived a few miles from Mac, just across the Tennessee state line.

After picking me up at the Memphis airport the following Monday morning, Mac took me to his upscale Germantown home to show off his den filled with game animals, most of which I couldn't name. The room looked like a museum. With a record-size pike, striped bass, and trout adorning one wall, a black bear grinned from the floor as we walked around it toward the center of the room. An enormous red grizzly bear stood on hind legs in the far corner posed to charge. In the opposite corner, a caribou with head held high displayed an antler rack the width of a basketball backboard.

Between the twinkling sets of eyeballs in the room and the sparkle from Mac's gold jewelry, I was beginning to think that there was far more profit in Davis & Geck thread than in CPR dummies... any day.

*   *   *

It was probably the easiest interview I'd ever had. Mac never shut up. Once I mentioned the fact that I had some experience calling on a particularly challenging account in the territory, he seemed genuinely relieved and began talking like I was already hired.

The hospital is one nearly every sales rep has struggled with at one time or another. Midwest University State Center at Lincoln & Elm (MUSCLE, for short) has been the source of ruin for many a representative. MUSCLE, one of the top teaching hospitals in the area, has, over the years, developed its own personality. You might say it is its own enigma.

From the dictionary we know the definition of "organism":

An individual form of life that is capable of growing, metabolizing nutrients, and reproducing.

That literally defines MUSCLE. Virtually unaffected by outside forces, it was a kingdom unto itself and the reps who tried to conquer it proceeded with great caution and a certain level of submission.

The white coats promenading the corridors of this prestigious institution were starched and crisp... every crease sharp, every collar pressed, and every ego inflated.

* * *

Near the end of my interview with Mac I glanced at my watch and realized I had endured nearly an hour of hunting stories before he even broached the subject of job duties or expectations. He handed me a brief questionnaire covering topics he had drawn up for the candidates. They were designed to see how a sales person might handle rejection.

Questions like: *How would you respond to an irate customer? Have you ever been banned from an account?* And believe it or not; *What would you say to a surgeon who tried your product and subsequently threw it at you?* I answered as best I could and handed it back. Mac glanced at the responses and promptly made a verbal offer.

I accepted on the spot... again.

The idea of leaving a small family-owned company like Anderson Medical and moving to a publicly held giant like American Cyanamid (the parent company of Davis & Geck) was intimidating. Manikins were one thing. Sterile fields, bloody hearts, and masked customers opened a whole new frightening world. But after reviewing the company's annual report, a few marketing brochures, and several clinical white papers from Mac, I was excited and convinced this was my new calling...needles and thread.

* * *

In the science of medicine, the discipline of surgery has represented the epitome of healthcare. There is no activity in the hospital that creates such high drama as that of the operative theater. The craft has consistently inspired people of all ages. The opportunity to improve life, provide a cure, or relieve suffering has been a hallmark for well over a century.

In a sense, surgery is universal. We are all under the knife when we are born, be it by Caesarian section or simply cutting and tying the umbilical cord. In the end, we ultimately succumb to the knife of the undertaker—when all our earthly problems are forever solved.

The mortality rate for surgical procedures is higher than most other medical interventions, so the prospect of any procedure can strike fear in the heart of the patient. Under the best circumstances, errors are possible—human and product. For that reason, medical device manufacturers will spend millions of dollars to equip sales representatives for the challenges of this uniquely demanding environment. If the product fails, a person could die. Patient safety and company liability are forever linked.

The week before I was to start training in New Jersey, Mac flew to St. Louis for dinner with Carol and me. As expected, the first two hours were filled with hunting and fishing stories which, after a while, began to run together. Mac had a habit of grinning whenever he spoke. As a result, "Greg" would come out like "Greeg" with a very long "e" sound.

Every few sentences he produced a quick chuckle, then moved on to the next point. Mac was the kind of guy who could be as comfortable behind a pawn shop counter as he was in scrubs—as long as the customer liked hunting. Most of the surgeons I worked with over the years had little time for hunting, and considered Mac's approach abrasive. It's all he talked about, and it was a little *too* upbeat for a busy, often exhausted surgeon. Ultimately, it cost him his job.

Over dessert, Mac told us the story of Cerise, an attractive young hire who gave every indication she was destined for success with Davis & Geck. She was a shoo-in, arguably due in part to her beauty, but also because of her proven leadership ability. She had sailed through three weeks of training, leading the class of fifteen aggressive ladder-climbers. Whether it was exams, role-plays, or wet labs where surgical technique was practiced, Cerise was consistently a champion.

During her first week in the field, Mac had arranged for the two of them to observe a procedure performed by a surgeon who had agreed to try the newest Davis & Geck suture. The scheduled case was a grueling operation called the 'Whipple' procedure. The formal name is *pancreaticoduodenectomy*. With so many letters and syllables, you figure it had to be a long and difficult procedure. According to a staff member at the hospital, the Whipple is the Cadillac of operations, one of the most complex abdominal procedures performed. It is highly specialized, often performed as the only hope of cure for a badly diseased pancreas. The gallbladder is removed, along with a portion of the bile duct, the duodenum (the curved tube at the end of the stomach), the head of the pancreas, and, when necessary, the lower part of the stomach. Once everything is re-routed and reconnected, the procedure may take as long as six hours—and a great deal of suture along the way.

The suture to be evaluated that morning was one that offered a new coating which made knot-tying faster and more manageable. It improved the "hand" or feel of the suture, a very important feature.

Linda, the head preceptor (the nurse managing the educational program for the department), directed Mac and Cerise to their respective locker rooms while staff enjoyed the six dozen donuts Cerise lugged in. Vaguely interested in why the reps came, most of the chatter in the lounge involved the prior weekend case load and who had been stuck on call.

Mac and Cerise met in the central core as they waited for the surgeons to appear at the scrub sink. Depending on the doctor and the procedure to be done, the time spent at the sink can be light and jovial, serious and silent, or anything in between. Done properly, the scrub takes a full five minutes; two minutes and thirty seconds per hand, which creates a captive audience for the sales rep. A good rep will quickly observe the surgeon's mood to determine approachability. Often with difficult or challenging cases, the physician will be intently focused on what is ahead and likely unreceptive.

That didn't matter to Mac. He thought the best way to a surgeon's heart was to talk about hunting—and keep talking about hunting. Cerise could see what was unfolding and felt the tension mount. She had observed one minor procedure in training where the atmosphere was casual and light-hearted. Not here. Mac was oblivious, relentlessly pounding away at the surgeon. She wanted him to back off, but he was the boss. She didn't want to make things worse for the doctor or, God forbid, the patient, who had just been put to sleep.

As the lead surgeon kicked the large lever beneath the scrub sink with his knee to shut off the water and held his dripping hands and forearms away from his body in a sterile pose, he turned to face Mac and Cerise as he backed into the room using his hips to open the door. Peering at the two visitors above his mask he simply said, "This shit better work."

Mac looked at Cerise and she could tell by his cheeks and the squint of his eyes that he was grinning under his mask. He offered a wink and nod of his head as if to say, 'now we've got him where we want him'. She quickly realized Mac's style was nothing like the technique she learned in her three weeks of sales training. He approached his prospects with the same strategy and tactics he used for hunting—get the cross hairs in place, fire, field dress, and enjoy the steaks. She wanted to say something but didn't know what.

The scrub nurse had finished prepping and draping the patient just before the doctors walked into the room. She assembled and arranged the dozens of sterile instruments in a strategic pattern on the Mayo stand, placing them in an order most likely to be requested by the surgeons, who were gowned, gloved, and stepping toward the side of the table. "Are we ready folks?" he sighed, knowing the tedium that faced them. The anesthesiologist gave a thumbs-up gesture, and the circulating nurse nodded, awaiting instructions from the team as the lead surgeon called for the scalpel: "Let's do it. Knife please."

The Whipple procedure is so extensive that it requires sterile preparation of an area just above the nipples, all the way down to the upper thighs, including the sides of the body down to the surface of the table itself. The incision is usually made midline, from the tip of the breastbone (sternum) to the pubic region. Once the initial opening is made, particularly in obese patients, the electrocautery devise becomes an essential tool for sealing the freshly severed blood vessels on the long, deep journey to the center of the abdomen.

Cerise got a head nod from Mac to move closer to the sterile field. He wanted to be sure she would be positioned within view of the surgeon at the moment the first D & G suture would be used. In that way, she could address any objections or receive accolades immediately.

Since the patient in this instance was obese and the vascular bed extensive, considerable cauterization was required to control bleeding. Each time the surgeon stepped on the electrical generator foot pedal causing a bug-zapper buzz, the small area of tissue surrounding the hand-held tip would not only char but produce plumes of pungent, noxious smoke that filled the room.

Researchers have identified no less than eighteen separate compounds in cauterized tissue smoke analyzed during various procedures. The compounds range from a colorless, harmless liquid called "nonanal" which is found in perfumes and flavorings, to "cyclohexanone," a powerful irritant and suspected carcinogen.

It is not surprising then, that precautionary measures have been taken in recent years to help minimize the amount of smoke produced during surgery by utilizing smoke evacuators and highly-engineered airflow systems.

On that Monday morning though, the Whipple procedure received no special attention. It was just another case in the OR. Cerise, however, had never been exposed to such much acrid smoke rising up from the opened abdomen and enveloping her puffy, bouffant hair cover. Her Ann Klein perfume was quickly being smothered by the raw, sweet, scorch of human flesh. Standing arms length from the patient, she couldn't avoid the wafting sizzle that looked like campfire smoke rising from deep inside the patient's core. Within minutes she began to taste the char.

Any interest Cerise may have developed in Whipple procedures, coated sutures, orders, or career success had suddenly been tossed, along with the contents of her stomach—right into her mask.

Mac couldn't believe it. Colorful dots of red, blue, yellow and brown began trickling down Cerise's neck from the bottom edge of her mask, the remnants of two Krispy Kreme sprinkle donuts. Cerise covered her mask with both hands as she turned with her head down, trying unsuccessfully to stop the flood. She trotted out of the room, never making eye contact.

That was the last he saw of her. She had headed straight to the women's locker room, quickly dressed, and took a cab straight to the airport. The rental car was left for Mac.

* * *

When he finished the story and asked for the dinner check, he paused and then chuckled. "Greeg," he said, "Are you *really* sure this is something you can handle... 'cause if it's not, now's the time to speak."

I briefly looked at Carol who said nothing, and responded, "No problem Mac."

That's when he shared one last detail.

Apparently, the largest account in the territory, the Midwest University State Center, was extremely unhappy with the products and services of Davis & Geck, to the extent that they formally exercised their option to cancel their contract by sending a certified letter (compliments of the attorneys) demanding the expulsion of all Davis & Geck products and representatives within 90 days. That meant whoever was hired as the suture rep would, in essence, be walking into a hornets' nest.

My noticeably troubled response was, "So what happened to the rep before me?"

Grinning wide, Mac chuckled and said, "Oh you'll meet. He'll be your trainer in New Jersey."

No problem Mac. No problem at all.

Chapter 10

I Once Was Blind

"He alone is an acute observer,
Who can observe minutely without being
observed."

Johann Kasper Lavater, German poet

GREGORY R. FROST, RRT

For as long as I can remember, I have been a student of life's more trivial elements and obscure details. These little things stick in my mind and serve as triggers allowing me to hold on to memories and recall faces and situations almost instantly. In sales it's a blessing. In life maybe not.

I can walk through the mall with my wife and see someone immediately recognizable as a former high school classmate, co-worker, or church member and say, "Look hon, there's so-and-so from high school, remember? He had a slight limp to the left when he walked to Mr. Irving's biology class. Remember?"

She'll shake her head saying, "I would *never* have recognized him in a million years. How do you *do* that?" I always tell her it's because I have the gift of 'heightened awareness' which helps me remember. Her reply is always the same, "Then how come you can't remember to match your pants with your shirt?" She can be funny.

There is an important truth in sales—more so in a specialized arena of surgical sales. It is the science of *physiognomy.* By definition, according to Merriam-Webster, physiognomy is: *"the art of discovering temperament and character from outward appearance,* or, *the inner character or quality revealed outwardly.*

This is a first-impressions approach to analyzing a prospect's make up and disposition. The reason this is so important in the OR is that everyone looks alike, or at least confusingly similar. The scrubs, shoe covers, scrub jackets, bouffant hair covers (let alone the masks) all serve to disguise and can cloud even the most perceptive eye.

A former co-worker, Dan Jennings, once told me that after being hired as a surgery department Business Manager for a local hospital, for the longest time he would feel uncomfortable on coffee breaks in the cafeteria. There was a small group of nurses in scrubs that usually took break at the same time. One nurse in particular would acknowledge him by name every day. Dan would nod, but basically ignored her. He thought she was from Labor & Delivery or Radiology, areas he had no reason to visit.

One morning she approached him with obvious exasperation. Squaring off to face him at his table with hands on her hips, she glared and said, "Jennings! Don't you know who I am?" She raised one hand to cover the lower half of her face and said, "Here!" Immediately, Dan recognized her as one of the RN's from the cardiothoracic team, a group that operated nearly every day in one of the two designated heart rooms. It was the mask that made the difference.

I learned to recognize nurses, techs, and surgeons by focusing on small details. Most wore their bouffant a certain way, having a flattened bubble shape depending on hair style. Some chose to wear the tighter style tie-down caps with a distinctive crest around the top.

Glasses were a dead give-away. Sometimes I would see a person in the cafeteria wearing a lab coat over scrubs, or dressed in street clothes. But after recognizing the glasses... an immediate "How you doing?' would follow with conversation.

* * *

By the time I had survived the ordeal in New Jersey and began traveling regularly to the Midwest University Health Center picking up (or cleaning up) where my predecessor had left off, I was observing and noting the nuances and gestures of the people that could help me. Find a champion, they would stress in training, someone who would advocate for you by helping you get in, get noticed, and get your product used.

OR access at Midwest, however, was not a problem. I was expected to be there two to three days each week, according to the terms of the contract. My job was to conduct suture inventories, maintaining adequate levels of both D & G *and* Ethicon suture. This meant going into every room, usually while a procedure was under way, and re-fill the custom suture racks and carts that the nurses pulled from. By the end of the day, I would generate a suggested order for the supply clerks to place.

Basically, I was an unpaid grunt for the hospital. But it worked both ways. They received the benefit of free labor, while I enjoyed unrestricted access to every surgeon and decision-maker on campus. This arrangement was described by the Chief of Orthopedic Surgery in the men's locker room one day when he asked, "A little like the fox guarding the hen house isn't it?" He wasn't far off.

*   *   *

I had much to learn. I naively thought being a blood relative of the founding family of the Storz Instrument Company would help catapult me to the leading ranks of the sales group. An uncle of mine, Eric Storz, had come from a family of craftsmen renowned for their knife-making ability. His great grandfather, Johann Jacob Storz, founded the company in Tuttlingen, Germany in 1792.

Adam Storz, grandson of Johann, took over the business, traveling to Paris to study the art of crafting fine surgical instruments. Along with his son, Charles, the decision was made to move the business to the United States. A few Master craftsmen who spoke no English were brought as well.

The company was based in St. Louis and peaked in the 60's and 70's. Eric and his wife, Celess, (my Aunt), were deeply entrenched in the St. Louis social scene, often attending gatherings or hosting parties at their beautiful Frontenac home for surgeons who demanded the very best.

Celess' role in the family business (aside from entertaining clients at her baby grand piano) was to gather two or three specific instruments of the surgeon's choice, line an attractive, gilded box with red felt and carefully secure the instruments inside. The surgeon's name was then engraved on the box, and the set would be promptly delivered to the hospital or physician's office, where it would be enthusiastically accepted.

Aunt Celess was paid $5.00 per box. This was a woman who had more money than she could count, yet loved to provide this simple, personal service for clients.

*   *   *

I had a golden opportunity, I thought, to parlay my connection with Storz into something special. Magical, it was not. For the most part, my boasting fell on deaf ears. Many of the professionals who may have had memories of the old days were either preoccupied with survival or simply not interested. The healthcare industry was re-shaping itself as a corporate, profit-driven business with managed care creating the highest level of competition.

As a result, I soon realized that if I was going to survive in such a hostile environment like the embittered Midwest State Center, I would have to provide a level of service that was sure to be noticed, which meant I had to live in the account. What did I have to lose?

Despite the fact we were being expelled from the account, I continued to show up every week, spending 50% or more of my time at the Health Center. I acknowledged each OR member by name whenever I could. With the area's low population and small town atmosphere, it was not uncommon to run into staff at restaurants or the mall any given evening. From the parking garage attendant to the laboratory technicians I passed in the hallways, I acknowledged them all. I hosted luncheons for the residents, brought candy to the secretaries, and provided donuts (less sprinkles) for the OR nearly every week. Gradually, they began to accept me.

Finally, I made it a point to *never* get in the way. They knew I was there but I wasn't viewed as a threat, and soon my visits became more social than selling.

When December rolled around, it was time for the suture bid, this time worth the better part of a million dollars. It was also the end of the road for D&G. The ninety days had come and gone, and we were to be officially booted from the account.

Headquarters in New Jersey, and Mac in-particular, couldn't believe we were sent an invitation to re-bid on the business. We all thought it was a system glitch which caused the accidental mailing of the bid by the hospital.

Miraculously, the decision to cancel the contract was reversed, and the final outcome revealed only minor changes. We held on to the business we'd enjoyed—a stunning 40% of the hospital's suture budget, which in turn represented over 60% of my entire territory sales volume, from a single account.

I was allowed to continue my weekly service schedule, which left Mac scratching his head. Things went so well that by the time my first anniversary had arrived, the surgery staff hosted a Bar-B-Q in my honor at the local city park. They were as astounded as I that D & G had maintained its market position and that I hadn't been chewed up and spit out. The real gratification came when the National Sales Manager, Jack Neal, flew to St. Louis to accompany me to the Health Center expressly for the purpose of, in his words, "kissing some ass" since we had survived the guillotine.

After meeting with the entire hospital management team, we were shaking hands and gathering our things in preparation to catch Jack's return flight. At that moment, the OR Director, Jim Barnes, a notoriously acerbic and fearlessly opinionated leader from the old school, stopped Neal in his tracks and said, "I want you to know something, Mr. Neal, and that is this. The *only* reason Davis & Geck is in this account today is because of Greg Frost. He has single-handedly turned the staff's attitude around and deserves the credit. Your corporate bull-shit didn't get you very far here... but this guy did."

PERMISSION TO OBSERVE

As we left the boardroom, I looked at Jack Neal and did my best Mac—a full, toothy grin and chuckle.

*　　*　　*

Now that the threat of losing one of my company's biggest accounts was no longer a factor, I was able to take a deep breath and service the hospital each week with a much greater sense of relief and ease. This allowed me the opportunity to spend more time observing cases I was interested in, and witnessed some of the most unusual procedures and techniques imaginable.

Surgeons are natural teachers. They love to instruct and use the operative suite as a classroom. As long as things flow smoothly in the procedure, the chance for questions, explanations, and close-up looks was always available. This is what I relished—freely moving from room to room where the opportunity to learn something new and fascinating waited behind every door.

As an officially designated Level I Trauma Center, the Health Center got it all. Everything from scratches and splinters to limb-ripping disasters were common. They were so busy, in fact, that plans were made to add another twelve suites in the main OR. This would help ease the burden of scheduling and minimize the bickering over what few rooms were available.

The Out-Patient Services area, on the other hand, was recently renovated and sparkled like a new car. They were the spoiled ones. With only eight rooms and a caseload of mostly elective procedures, the staff enjoyed the luxury of controlling the flow as they saw fit.

I typically started Monday mornings in out-patient surgery, mainly because it was near the parking garage and on the way to the main OR. The mood was usually light and it gave me a chance to get my thoughts together for whatever lay ahead in the OR.

GREGORY R. FROST, RRT

Despite the fact we maintained our share of the business, the level of complaints from surgeons about product quality issues or performance remained the same... disturbingly high. Some were legitimate, like a multi-pack of five sutures which only contained four. Or an $850 box of heart suture (about the diameter of a human eyelash), which had passed the expiration date for guaranteed sterility. These were relatively minor issues which were quickly addressed. I would fill out the Customer Complaint form, replace the product in question on the spot from my sample car stock, and usually throw in an extra box to help assuage their grief.

A few of the staff simply lived to complain, and made it a priority to keep the reps in a place of subservience. I had the opportunity early in my career to work closely with the senior St. Louis rep that had been with the company over a decade. He had gained great wisdom from spending so much time putting out the fire of complaints.

I once asked how he handled objection and criticism when a genuinely ticked-off surgeon decided to vent his or her wrath. He said he nodded a lot in agreement and didn't really respond to the tirades. He would patiently wait, offer quick thanks for the feedback, and walk the other direction.

"Damn surgeons," he'd mumble "can't find their socks in the morning but they'll remember a D&G stitch that broke ten years ago."

* * *

Before the renovation of the OR, access to the scheduling desk (the main beehive of activity and the critical access point for sales reps) was through a single set of scratched and badly dented electric doors just outside the visitor elevators on the third floor. Anyone in street clothes could hit the red button on the wall and venture where few dared (who hadn't first been drugged).

Once inside, the contrast of light and dark, clean and dirty, fresh and not so fresh was a striking attribute of the

MUSCLE operating rooms. The main center corridor was dimly lit, but white light flooded from each of the small windows mounted in the doors of the rooms - like rays beaming down from heaven.

Walking down the corridor toward the scheduling desk with my sales bag, polished shoes and pin-striped suit, I was an easy target. Even before changing into scrubs I was often approached with something like, "Hey Greg, you've got a big problem... go see Ellen," or "Dr. Miller is screaming about that new suture. He had trouble over the weekend and wants to see you in Room 7." This is when thick skin pays off.

* * *

One of the more memorable procedures I witnessed was a plastic surgery case involving a penile implant, the likes of which could have been in the Guinness Book of World Records.

The basis for the procedure, of course, is to treat the condition of impotence, with the ultimate goal of resuming some degree of sexual activity.

Rosemary was the nurse scrubbed in that day, and I'm sure she noticed that I came into the room more than I usually did to check inventory. The plastics cases were almost exclusively performed with competitive product, since the Chairman of the Plastic Surgery Department happened to be an active board member of Ethicon. So I had little reason to be in the room. But the remarkable size of this particular implant and corresponding host tissue had created a sense of wonder and amazement that drew me in... again and again.

It may be an exaggeration, but as the doctor carefully stitched up the incision with his forearm resting on the patient's abdomen, were it not for the blue sleeve of his sterile gown, I would have had trouble deciphering which was which. The thing was walloping, more massive than the one Nate flung around the house that fateful day of the neighbor's visit.

I once saw a PBS or cable special a few years back featuring an obscure African or South American tribe that practiced the art of penile lengthening. An old tribesman demonstrated the technique for the camera crew. He first reached for a two foot long stick about the diameter of a one inch gas pipe. He had spent hours smoothing the bark of the stick for the exercise he was about to perform.

Spreading the grass of his skirt, he reached down and began to wrap his penis (starting at the tip, of course) and slowly rolled it around the stick, working it up toward his abdomen. Like hauling in the string of a stubborn kite, the whole thing ended up looking like an impaled, burnt cinnamon roll. The old master grinned at the camera and babbled some tribal chant.

After holding the position for several seconds, he slowly unrolled and began to laugh. Throwing the stick aside, he placed his hands on his hips, proudly revealing what must have been a source of absolute joy for his wives.

Until that day in out-patient surgery, I thought nothing could match the guy in the jungle. As I dressed in the locker room and headed for the main OR, I couldn't shake the image of that implant from my mind. I was troubled on so many levels.

Later, I took a break from inventory for some lunch and saw Rosemary with a few other nurses in the cafeteria. They had already finished lunch and were headed upstairs. Before they stepped in the elevator, I scooted away from my table to catch her and ask the obvious. "Rosie," I whispered, as I walked toward the group and gestured for her to wait. The others went on ahead. "You know that reconstruction case you were on this morning?"

She said, "Oh yeah, the implant. Big 'un wasn't it?"

That broke the ice for me so I probed ahead. "I've got to tell you, Rose, that's the biggest wanker I have *ever* seen. Why in the world would anybody want one that big?"

Without batting an eye she waved her hand saying, "Oh, that's easy... "It was a woman." And off she went to catch the next elevator, leaving me standing speechless next to the salad bar.

So there it was. This monumental symbol for manhood that flopped like a killer whale before my eyes... was owned by a woman, named Greta, no less. Had I paid closer attention to the scheduling board before waltzing into the room, I would have seen that this was a transgender case in its final stages.

The out-patient supervisor later told me that what I had seen was not unusual. The grafting process begins by deliberately super-sizing the member so that it may later be "sculpted down" to a more realistic size, shape, and overall appearance.

Once the entire implant procedure is complete, the last stitch removed, and the tissues have fully healed, there is no doubt that Greta will have ample reason to grin—just like the guy in the jungle.

—Chapter 11—

Blaze

"Some say the world will end in fire,
Some say in ice."

Robert Frost

Permission to Observe

Of all the hours spent observing procedures only two give me pause. One is cataract surgery. Whenever an ophthalmic case was underway, I would avoid looking directly at the patient's exposed and vulnerable eye. There was something about the steel clamps holding the lids open while the eye blankly stared that made me squirm. I realize the eyeball is fully anesthetized and the patient feels nothing. Still, the sight was unnerving. Fortunately, the team leader for the ophthalmic cases managed most of the suture, so I didn't have to go in the room very often. I could live with that.

The cases I found even more troubling than ophthalmic repairs were burn cases. They usually involved debridement—the removal of dead, decayed, or potentially infectious tissue in order to expose healthier raw flesh to facilitate healing.

Burns are normally classified as first, second, or third degree. However, according to the Abbreviated Burn Severity Index (a scale used to evaluate injury and probability of survival), there is actually a *fourth* degree, or a 'char burn'. This is a full-thickness burn that has penetrated all layers of soft tissue with damage to bones, joints, tendons, muscles, vessels, and nerves. Fourth degree causes deep tissue loss, and healing may never be complete.

The fact that burn patients experience such intense pain while grappling with feelings of doom, helplessness, and hopelessness, can make the treatment especially stressful for the caregivers. Great care must be taken to avoid any appearance, signal, or body language indicating distaste or shock which could be perceived in the eyes of the patient as yet another message of rejection.

Cancer is devastating. It can take a tremendous toll on the appearance of victims. Serious burns, on the other hand, reach a new dimension in fear and self-repugnance. The results are hard to disguise and often irreversible.

GREGORY R. FROST, RRT

Burns scar the victim inside *and* out. When someone has sustained a serious burn over a significant percentage of body area, the physiological response may prevent the body's temperature regulating mechanism from operating properly. Tremendous amounts of heat are released through what used to be an effective layer of insulation—the skin. Because of the likelihood of hypothermia, a debridement procedure will prompt the OR staff to take extraordinary measures to prepare the room environment for the taxing and distressing treatment that follows.

* * *

Robert Paul Hutchins had farmed his 280 acres of land in the adjacent county for as many of his sixty-six years as he could remember. Known throughout the county as Junior, he worked the land as his father did before him. There was a legacy when you farmed, a certain honor to be upheld. Pride was a natural trait and it permeated all areas of life in the Hutchins' home.

None of Junior's family ever had much use for the Midwest University State Center at Lincoln & Elm, avoiding doctors, hospitals, and banks for that matter. Most of the everyday injuries and illnesses could be managed at home with a little witch hazel, a tightly wrapped cloth, and a generous swig of Jack Daniels. Hutchins thought that if he drove into town for every little health problem, he'd never have the time he needed to farm the huge trinity of crops: corn, soybeans, and winter wheat. Junior figured that when bad things happened, as they often did, you just fixed them and kept going.

Junior never expected to retire. But he thought as long as the weather held through the planting seasons, and the crops came in on time, his four children would have supper every night and a chance for a decent future. The first two plantings, corn in early April, and soybeans in late May, were in. Just about the time the soybean plants started to turn a beautiful shade of yellow-gold, it was time to get the winter wheat in. Junior always targeted the first of October to get his crop underway.

It was a busy time of the year for the Hutchins clan. The kids had begun school and the time to harvest was imminent. The wheat wouldn't wait much longer. Junior had a lot on his mind, but always seemed to. He took his job seriously, trying his best to read rural journal articles and keep abreast of new trends in farming. There always seemed to be insects to battle, weather to fret over, and equipment that needed fixing. Harvest time was always busy and with everything that had to be done, it was easy to overlook some things and get a little careless.

Late afternoon on the first Monday of October, Junior was wrapping up the last of his chores. He was anxious to get back to the house for supper, a little Jack Daniels, and spending time with his family. The day had been full, readying everything for planting the wheat on Tuesday. Junior knew he would spend the majority of the day on his prized 1950 Persian Orange, thirty horsepower Allis-Chalmers "WD" series tractor. That meant he would need a full tank of fuel.

Handling the old tractor wasn't a challenge. He had negotiated the tortuous hills and creek beds for years, and never once experienced, or even came close to a rollover, the main cause of farm worker accidental death.

Junior had a habit of enjoying a brief smoke at the end of the day, just before stepping into the house to greet Claire and the kids. He decided to savor a filtered Marlboro before the last job, filling up the tractor.

Some things were so predictable, he thought; seedtime, waiting, worrying, harvest. It was the cycle of rural life. But by the end of the day, the Hutchins' cycle of life had been dramatically interrupted. Shortly into the task of filling the tractor's tank, Junior brushed what he'd thought to be a bug from the front of his overalls. It was a tiny, glowing ember from his just-finished Marlboro. Life suddenly became unpredictable.

* * *

OR Supervisor Lynn Fowler said Junior's was the worst case she had seen. He sustained third and fourth degree burns covering the entire front surface of his body with extensive deep tissue damage to the mid-section. According to her explanation, the fuel first splashed Junior at the instant of the explosion and immediately set fire to his clothing and skin.

A colleague, who has taught physical science for several years, later told me that the unpredictable nature and volatility of combustible fuel is nothing to take for granted. "That stuff does funny things," he would say, shaking his head. He went on to share the story of a close friend of who had sustained similar burns.

The friend, Craig Lacey, was in the process of clearing brush on his father's property early one summer. After creating a perimeter around the pile with kerosene, he (like Junior) got in a hurry. He decided to use gasoline to create a thirty foot trail or wicking path to the pile. The gas, he thought, would serve as an accelerant to speed the burn and get the job done quicker.

The combination of chemicals and sudden shift in wind was a recipe from hell. Once he had set the gas can aside and pulled out a cigarette lighter to ignite the trail, the spark caused an immediate explosion that catapulted him into a nearby pond.

The lighter melted into his hand.

Lacey found himself in a semi-reclined position with the left side of his body, neck, and face submerged in cold, green liquid. The scum-coated pond water had trickled into his mouth causing him to choke and rouse. He later recounted that the first thing he saw after regaining consciousness was a busy group of small frogs and minnows hungrily feasting on the loosened flesh of his forearm.

After being air-lifted to a hospital, a device like a power washer was used for the initial debridement of the sloughed skin. According to Lacey, the "wash" was done without the benefit of anesthesia. His screams were heard throughout the Burn Unit.

* * *

By the time I checked in for my suture inventory rounds on Tuesday, Junior was undergoing a debridement procedure in Room 8—the infamous Burn Room. It was here that I saw the most depressing and troubling cases I would ever encounter. During my weekly visits, I checked the suture stock only when I knew the room was not being used. If a procedure was underway, the temperature of ninety degrees combined with a relative humidity of thirty percent made it unbearable to stay for any length of time. The room was its own inferno. If summoned to Room 8 for any reason, I would immediately have to change scrubs afterward. Wringing wet and stinking of charred flesh, I would strip them off as fast as possible hoping I wouldn't carry the sickening stench with me.

Emergency physicians, trauma surgeons, and staff members who day-in and day-out save lives may garner their own glory. But in my mind, it's the burn team that transcends the very idea of *first do no harm*. Few procedures require such presence of mind and relentless optimism. Inherently, the role contains elements of risk with far-reaching consequences for the patient, who may view the caregiver as both savior and slaughterer.

Junior must have thought this, because every few days, like clockwork, his chest, abdomen, groin and thighs were completely stripped of the crust-forming layer of flesh. This was done to expose more viable tissue and promote healing from the inside out. The ghastly procedure, called an escharectomy, can be likened to peeling off an enormous, full-thickness body scab.

Along with the unforgiving climate in the room, other special considerations are required. Operating during the night, for example, is not uncommon. Burn patients desperately need fluids, so by calling in or scheduling the team for a night procedure, the patient's critical daytime schedule for oral intake goes uninterrupted.

A friend who practices general surgery in a small midwestern town was familiar with burn cases during his training. He once commented on his experience during residency, "The burn patient challenge presents a horrendous site and smell. You need to override your emotions to stay focused on what needs to be done; the ABC's—airway, breathing, circulation. You don't ever forget those cases."

Dr. William Osler, founder of the Johns Hopkins School of Medicine, delivered a stirring speech to the 1889 graduating class at the University of Pennsylvania titled, *Aequanimitas*, which is the Latin origin of 'equanimity' or staying cool in the face of great peril. He admonished the new graduates with this advice, "The first essential is to have your nerves well in hand; stand up bravely, even against the worst."

*   *   *

I wasn't very brave that awful October day. I was walking past Room 8 on my way to watch an open heart procedure. The chief of cardiothoracic surgery had agreed to try my company's suture designed specifically for vascular repairs. We had also patented a special duel-edge sharpening process for the needles. This allowed the user to pierce the tissue effortlessly, cutting on both sides as it slices through the tiny vessel wall.

I heard my name called from the doorway. Reluctantly, I changed direction and turned to see what they wanted. The circulating nurse was waving her hand for me to come her way. Hopefully, it was something simple. A quick check of the suture rack and I'd be right back out the door. Lynn had told me earlier that morning what to expect so I was hoping to avoid the room altogether, making it my last check of the day.

Opening the door, I was immediately blasted by intense heat and moisture. At center stage was Junior. Naked, blackened, and lying on his back, he lay motionless as his lower abdomen and penis was being scraped clean. Speechless, I stood in the oppressive heat and watched as the team carefully sculpted Junior's groin down to a glistening red-pink color. I jerked when I heard the surgeon say, "Hey your suture is pretty good. I think we need to have it available for these tough cases."

That was enough. Nodding a thank-you, I quickly turned to get to the nearest water fountain. Pulling off the mask and swishing some water in my mouth to rinse the taste of the air, I hoped I wouldn't ever have to see, smell, or *taste* another debridement.

*　　*　　*

Not surprisingly, Junior's family ended up selling their place, moving to a small house closer to town and doctors. Although he survived the explosion, he would never be able to maintain the farm. His life was now tethered to the hospital, specialists, rehab appointments, skin treatments, and countless reconstructive surgeries that loomed.

I saw Junior and Claire one last time, about seven months after the accident. I had recently been promoted to the mid-west Regional Specialist for Minimally Invasive Surgery (MIS), and had moved away from suture, focusing on instrument sales instead.

It was late in the afternoon on a sunny day in May. Junior should have been on his tractor. Instead, he was riding in a wheelchair, with Claire straining to push him across the thick lobby carpeting of the Health Center toward the atrium elevators that led to the Plastic Surgery Clinic.

Had I not overheard his name in the lobby as I headed for the bank of pay phones, I wouldn't have recognized him. Bandaged on both arms and chest, he breathed through the tracheostomy tube permanently placed in his neck. An oxygen cylinder was strapped to the chair. His breathing was labored; his eyes were glassy and watered constantly.

As the couple slowly wheeled past the pay phone where I sat, we exchanged an awkward glance. I couldn't let them go without saying *something*, but what? All I could think of was "Aren't you Mr. Hutchins?"

Claire stopped the wheelchair and looked at me in a numb, tired way. "Do we know you?"

"I was in the O.R. the day of the accident," I said proudly. "I was the one managing the suture." Hoping they would associate my product with a successful outcome, they would somehow acknowledge me as a member of the team. I realized the moment I said it that it was self-serving, and wished I could take back my pointless words.

Claire nodded slightly as she again began pushing the chair. Junior was silent. I had run out of things to say and it was getting uncomfortable. Wishing the two of them a good day would have been cruel and insulting. So I just stood there. Just before we separated, Junior raised an arm to plug the opening of his trach tube so he could speak.

He strained to put just two words together: "Lucky you."

* * *

It's unlikely that Paul, one of the writers of the New Testament, had Junior Hutchins in mind when he wrote about the great mystery of the body's ultimate healing; the resurrection, or how the law of sowing and reaping applies not just to farmers, but to us all.

Still, I can only hope that patients like Junior will, through these disasters, somehow be drawn to a place of peace knowing that the sting of death and the horrors of life will ultimately be swallowed up in victory:

Permission to Observe

Behold, I tell you a mystery; we shall not all sleep, but we shall all be changed.

I Corinthians 15

—Chapter 12—

Night Harvest

"There seems to be no calamity overtaking man,
That cannot be rendered merchantable."

Herman Melville
Redburn; His First Voyage

PERMISSION TO OBSERVE

Years ago, I read the novel *Redburn* by Herman Melville. As he described his travels between voyages, he takes the reader to a peculiar landmark near the Liverpool shipping docks, the old Church of St. Nicholas. Below the sanctuary, where the long, slow peal of bells filled the hall, lay stack upon stack of decomposing bloated bodies. The church was one of the few places of worship in the area at the time, and quite possibly the only active sanctuary containing a mausoleum. Melville's description reads:

In the basement of the church is a Dead House. Like the Morgue in Paris, where bodies of the drowned are exposed until claimed by their friends, or till buried at the public charge.

I was told that standing rewards are offered for the recovery of persons falling into the docks; so much, if restored to life, and a less amount if irrecoverably drowned.

I used to see a crowd gazing through the grim iron grating of the door, upon the faces of the drowned within. And once, when the door was opened, I saw a sailor stretched out, stark and stiff, with the sleeve of his frock rolled up, and showing his name and date of birth tattooed upon his arm. It was a sight full of suggestions; he seemed his own head-stone.

Struck by the relentless search for bodies, Mehlville calls them 'rag-pickers' who constantly pried about the docks early each morning for bodies—all in the name of commerce.

For then, the night-harvest has ripened.

I too have labored in the night harvest. Though never clawing my way through dock pillars or scavenging the surf, my method of procuring human tissue for transplant involved a much more refined approach—one of gourmet dining, expensive wines, tickets for sporting events, and other gifts for services rendered.

Specifically, my new job as Region Manager for a prominent tissue bank was to obtain the raw material required for the production of precision-engineered bone graft implants (allograft) commonly used in reconstructive surgery.

In other words... I bought dead bodies.

We really didn't *buy* them, since the trafficking or purchase of human tissue in the United States is deemed illegal. We did, however, through our national network of fee-for-service recovery agencies, procure vast amounts of human tissue from donors. Bones for the production of grafts were used to repair sports injuries and other degenerative conditions; heart valves were obtained for underdeveloped or diseased hearts; and of course skin, to help mend the superficial layers of the body.

These are some of the obvious *good* things developed with donated tissue. Unfortunately, much of it was (and is) discarded, ending up in biological waste incinerators. There are many uses for human tissue, and more than one motive.

* * *

The organization I worked for remains one of the dominant players in the world of tissue processing and allograft production. Their expertise is in the manufacture of grafts used in sports medicine—things like bone screws, pins, tendon pieces, and refined bone paste, which, when surgically implanted, helps speed the entire healing process.

Torn rotator cuffs, severed anterior cruciate ligaments (ACL), and the repair of shattered bones are injuries often requiring additional support of the body's own skeletal framework.

The company, along with others in the billion dollar tissue industry, has successfully provided countless grafts, organs, and implantable devices for surgeons around the world. Saving lives and supporting families for nearly half a century, they are not without their flaws.

Having survived a career with Davis & Geck, I felt sufficiently tempered by the politics of the OR to embrace this mysterious and controversial world of tissue banking.

The corporate culture and environment at National Tissue Services, LLC, however, turned out to be unlike any organization I have ever been part of.

It began with interview day.

*   *   *

My prospective boss, Dan Signorelli, had invited me to join him on a connecting flight from Atlanta, where we would then proceed to the NTS corporate office in Florida. Its proximity to the swamps added yet another dimension to an already strange opportunity.

Dan was a registered nurse who, like me, had decided to abandon the patient care side of healthcare and plunged into the arena of medical device manufacturing—a world of profit-driven quotas and relentless pressure from board executives to meet and exceed mandated numbers. It is known as satisfying shareholders and in this particular case, framed within the ghastly and bizarre context of death and dismemberment.

We touched down around noon. Once we'd grabbed the luggage, Dan used the drive time to headquarters to begin my indoctrination by meticulously explaining the complex relationship between non-profit organ procurement organizations known as OPO's (or the *good* guys), and for-profit tissue processors like NTS (the *bad* guys).

All OPO's across the country are regional, federally-designated industry gatekeepers who purposely position themselves as kings in their fiefdoms. It could be compared with the California gold rush—staking a claim to a territory which then becomes the sole property of the claimant. Under no circumstances then, could a profit-hungry technology-driven company (like NTS) *dare* set foot in an OPO's area without experiencing intense scrutiny, veiled threats, and effectively orchestrated pressure. Basically, it was an old-fashioned, all-American battleground. Instead of gold, the prize is bodies.

Dan and I pulled into the parking lot of what appeared to be a typical office park with small buildings and connecting sidewalks like thousands elsewhere. Hopping out of his black convertible sports car in the spot next to us was Patrick Graham, NTS's founder and Chief Executive Officer. Pat was late for an important meeting. He had just returned from a month-long sailing trip in the Caribbean and stopped only long enough for Dan to introduce me as the new Midwest candidate. A quick handshake and he was off to the meeting. I remember being surprised that he could afford to spend that much time away from his business. It didn't take long to figure out that Pat could afford quite a bit.

As we walked around the corner of the main building with the NTS logo, we crossed campus toward the center area where the sidewalks merged. There, smack in the middle of the courtyard was a circus tent of huge proportion. Staked securely with ropes strong enough to handle the warm Florida breezes, the canvas shielded hundreds of attendees in rows of folding chairs (many in scrubs and lab coats) with table upon table of catered gourmet food and drink.

The image reminded me of a loud gospel revival meeting. Rather than a sweating preacher in a dark suit riling up the crowd, the speaker at the podium was a relaxed ex-hippie with a long gray pony tail. As he spoke, Pat Graham arrived and took his front row seat marked "Reserved." He was all smiles and anxious to become part of the festivities. The NTS monthly shareholder meeting was now officially underway.

We stood just inside the tent opening and watched it unfold.

Dan leaned over and whispered, "The guy with the ponytail and the Hawaiian shirt is Stinson... the CFO." He went on to say, "According to his figures, sales are up roughly 400% over last quarter."

PERMISSION TO OBSERVE

Not too shabby for bones.

Following the business meeting, people began to scatter. Dan managed to catch a few managers and introduced me before going to the main building for a facility tour.

My personal guide was Paul Enlowe, a trim, dark-skinned man of Bahamian descent who was proud of his heritage and just as proud of working for NTS. Besides Dan and me, he was the only other person wearing a suit. The January humidity in Florida was oppressive, but the sweat rolling down Paul's puffy cheeks didn't bother him. After a damp hand shake, we began the tour.

*　　*　　*

As we walked through the halls of the processing building, I couldn't help but notice the fact that although eloquent and well groomed, Paul exhibited a few cultural vocabulary nuances. Tissue was pronounced 'tee-shoe' and the word donor came out a lot like 'donner'... as in Donner Pass.

Paul was assigned the demanding role of overseeing Medical Records - the department responsible for ultimately determining the suitability of donated tissue... the 'process-it-or-pitch-it' department. Tremendous pressure from upper management was placed on the Medical Records department whenever tissue inventories began to backlog. At one point, more than five years worth of donated bone, tendons, total joints, and skin had accumulated and was being stored in an obscure, unmarked closet known as The Dark Room.

The containers within this room held the donated body parts of Mr. Jones, Mrs. Smith, Miss Green, and countless other people—young and old. Unfortunately, information from the medical record of each donor was incomplete. It could have been something as minor as a single physical history detail not supplied by the next-of-kin. Or it's possible that additional information surfaced *after* the tissue recovery had already been performed, in which case the tissue would be rendered questionable, and not yet process worthy. In other words, worthless.

With a wary eye, I peered into the room as Paul unlocked the door and flipped on the lights. There, I saw row upon row of stacked Tupperware-type boxes, each labeled with strips of torn duct tape, stating the donor's name, date of recovery, and status of the paperwork. All read "Pending Medical Release." The final scene in Raiders of the Lost Ark immediately came to mind, where the Ark of the Covenant is casually wheeled down a long aisle, only to be swallowed up in the bowels of a government warehouse.

But what also came to mind was the question of how donor families would feel if they knew their loved one's tissue was homeless—packed in some cold, dark warehouse room. As we stepped away from the door, I asked if he thought these tissues would ever be viable and used as the donor or family intended. He snapped off the light, shrugged his shoulders and turned to head down the hall to the processing lab. I didn't know how to interpret his response.

The processing lab was set up in assembly line fashion with separate rooms, all viewable from the main hall by way of thick, plate glass windows. The first area was the intake section or the 'dirty' room. Here, we stood watching hooded technicians in full surgical garb with face shields, pull pink, dripping bones from recovery coolers and organize them on a long table. Identification and verification of donor was next with the tagging of each piece.

Great care was taken in prepping the long bones (scraping off the excess soft tissue) then sectioning each with a commercial band-saw. When the long bones were cut, the image seemed surreal in that I heard no sound coming from the saw. The thick glass prevented any sound from one area to another. Although I couldn't hear the whining saw blade, I cringed as I saw specks of bone and marrow spray the face shield of the technician like fine, wet carpenter sawdust.

The next room was the tooling station. Here, a worker would carefully wedge each of the small sections of long bone between two polished armatures mounted on the bed of a sophisticated lathe. The lathe took up half the room and was a completely automated operation. Once programmed, the machine took over while the operator stood by. The precision blades coupled with a proprietary software program created fine, smooth threads of exact dimensions. The end result was a screw that could be sterilized and later used for the repair of a broken hip, a spinal fusion, or a delicate facial reconstruction.

The climax of the tour was just around the corner. I could hear the excitement build in Paul's voice as he led me to the last room at the end of the hall. He stopped, took a deep breath and turned to face me as if to add drama. He said that what we were about to see in the next room was undoubtedly the greatest advancement to ever emerge within the world of tissue banking. The final stage of processing is perhaps the most critically important step of all.

This is where the cleansing of the tissue graft takes place. Up until the time NTS patented the unique process, tissue preparation had consisted mainly of employing various types of detergents, mixtures of solvents, some aggressive scrubbing, and a lot of finger-crossing in the hope that the soon-to-be-implanted tissue would not prove to be contaminated or worse, a carrier of disease.

Sterility had not been possible due to the difficulty of penetrating the bone to its core with detergents. This is an absolutely essential step in order to remove all traces of blood, because the life is in the blood, and the blood is the primary harbinger of disease.

The NTS process could do it.

As we stood at the viewing window, what appeared in the final room was a pair of shiny, stainless steel biscuit-shaped containers on stands, each about the size of a clothes basket.

These represented the holy grail of the industry... the million dollar NTS washing machines—guaranteed to sterilize tissue and render it safe for implantation, a claim no company had ever been able to make. Yet despite the seemingly obvious marketing advantage over all other tissue processors, NTS was still viewed as the maverick organization with motives solely based on profit and greed... *the bad guys.*

Because of this technological edge, the mud-slinging from other processors and non-profit agencies (especially OPO's) was disparaging and often furious. This was an incredibly passionate and hostile battle for which I was being recruited.

* * *

By the end of interview day, my mind was swimming and I was physically drained. I really didn't know what to think about entering such a strange industry and unusual company. Still, I had one last meeting to go—an interview with the company vice president, Tim Matthews. My hope was that by the end of the meeting I would be comfortable with the thought of earning a living and supporting my family by collecting cadavers.

The time spent with Tim was thankfully brief, all of 5 minutes. Following a quick handshake he asked what I thought of the place and what my opinion was regarding the tissue industry. Before I had a chance to answer, he said, "Greg, think of it like this—we are not ghouls, nor are we grave robbers. Rather, we are in the business of harvesting *donated* tissue to produce transplant grafts that change lives for the better—and forever. You would be providing a highly valued service. And as far as the other guys in the industry are concerned, well, we're all just one big incestuous family anyway."

He looked at me and said, "So. How much you think you need?"

That was my offer.

I threw out a number without giving it any thought and I was hired.

On my flight back to St. Louis I played the day over and over in my mind; the sailor CEO with more money than all of us, the rousing revival tent meeting with the hip CFO, the eerie processing tour, and the casual attitude toward blood, gore, and the dead.

The dead, who would soon be helping me live. The more I thought the more my head throbbed. The idea of making a cushy living as a result of the misfortune and loss of others shouldn't bother me. After all isn't that the essence of healthcare? People get sick, they get help, and then they get billed. Doctors do it. That's how it works.

For decades, tissue banking provided a comfortable living for its own. My three years with NTS proved to be one of the highest paid and most visible jobs of my career. It was also the most troubling. This visibility allowed me the opportunity to establish relationships with some of the most unusual people God has ever placed on this earth.

Take for example Alberto Sanchez. "Bert" as he was known, was a lean-built man with a thin mustache and dark hair. In his early thirties and happily married with two daughters, he left South America with the hope of studying transplant medicine in the United States. The closest he came was getting a job in a hospital surgery department as a nursing assistant in the cardiothoracic specialty.

It was there that he became an expert in anatomy, and was soon recruited by NTS as a tissue recovery specialist. He was ultimately named the NTS Corporate Trainer.

Bert spoke with a thick, barely discernible accent. He tended to roll his r's like Ricardo Montalban who touted the

1975 Chrysler C*orrr*doba with its soft, C*orrr*inthian leather. Whenever he called to discuss donor opportunities with the recovery agencies I was assigned, he'd always start by saying something perky like, "Hey G*rrr*eg, deese is Bert. How you bean anyhow?"

Bert was arguably the king of recoveries. Although the company would contract with various recovery agencies across the country to obtain raw tissue, Bert was available for local assignments in a pinch. He would work anytime, day or night to perform any type of recovery. The guy was fascinated with the work and prided himself in both accuracy and speed. He also made a considerable amount of money for his services.

The word at the office water cooler was that once a donor was properly positioned, draped and prepped, Bert could remove eight long bones, two hips, both Achilles tendons, plus an assortment of veins all in less than an hour; to use his words, "skin-to-skin in 38 minutes."

He once told me about his most ghastly and troubling recovery, one where he was asked to remove tissue, bones, and skin from four victims of a fatal vehicle crash on a holiday weekend. It was a vacationing family; mom, dad (who had been driving) and two young children. Bert said the sight of the four horribly broken bodies in one small room—naked, lined up on stretchers and absolutely still was almost too much to look at—even for him.

* * *

About two weeks after being hired, I returned to headquarters as the new Midwest Region Manager for NTS. Dan had scheduled a week of meetings and orientation as I prepared to visit the recovery agencies I would be responsible for. Since there were only four managers, we each covered a large geographic area. Mine included Missouri, Illinois, Nebraska, South Dakota, Oklahoma, Indiana, Tennessee, Alabama, Michigan, Texas, upstate New

York, and New York City. I spent a great deal of time in the air... thinking.

Orientation was paperwork and meetings for the most part. Dan couldn't join me that particular week, so I was on my own bouncing from office to office learning the operation and getting acquainted with the flow of people and paperwork. If a donor happened to crop up that week, I was slated to tag along with the recovery team as an observer.

I also had the opportunity late in the week to visit the Call Center, where highly trained communication specialists called "Requesters" would contact prospective donor families in the hope of gaining consent. I cannot imagine having a job like that. Repeated, intrusive phone calls to grieving and inconsolable families would not be the way I'd like to spend my afternoons.

The one and only consent call I was able to listen to was with a woman who had just lost her husband to a rare disease. Since he was under 75, had no reported cancers or other specific conditions which would preclude tissue suitability, he was a prime candidate for donation.

The Requester, a young girl in her twenties named Sheila, was fresh out of college and had a soft, irresistible southern accent. She had prepped me thoroughly before patching me into the system with a head-set, stating that I needed to be absolutely silent and resist any urge to speak. This was the critically important call.

I slipped on the head-set and listened to the ring tones along with Sheila. The donor's wife, Mrs. Jean Gadson, answered after four rings. She was clearly distraught and confused. Her voice quivered and she sobbed often. Understandable, since her husband of more than forty years had passed away unexpectedly and one of her first phone calls was from an organization asking for parts of his body—her life-long partner, Arthur.

The conversation was agonizing. I could only listen a few minutes. When she told Sheila that she wasn't at all sure she could continue living without him, I quietly slid the head-set off nodding at Sheila, who was doodling on a scratch pad. She offered a quick smile as I slipped out of the sound-proof cubicle.

It was late in the day Thursday and I was scheduled to fly back to St. Louis on Friday. My head pounded, I was hungry, and I felt distressed about the non-stop talk of death, donation, and dollars. By this time, I was ready to be home. I wasn't disappointed that Bert had not gotten a call for a recovery. It was just as well. I was exhausted and suffered from information overload.

I told the Vice President's secretary that I was heading for the hotel to grab a bite and that I would check in with her in the morning before heading to the airport.

Fortunately, no one was available to have dinner with me that final night, so I wouldn't have to talk more about death and donation. I went to my room to shower, unwind, and order room service.

* * *

The phone rang at 2:09 a.m.

It was Bert.

"*Grrr*eg", he said. "We got one! You wanna go?"

At first, I thought I overslept and was late for the office. But it was still dark. "Hmm, what?" I mumbled.

Bert repeated, "Well, what you say... you up to it?"

Finally I grasped what he was asking and responded in a dry, cracking voice, "What time does it start?" I asked, not realizing that it *couldn't* start until we got there.

"We gonna pick you up in 15 minutes. Got to get supplies first."

"Sure," I said. "I'll be in the lobby."

NTS had rented a locker near the hotel for storing recovery supplies. Anyone who happened to be on call had keys to the locker and was able to pick up the necessary kit(s) en- route to the donor.

The kits contained several items used during a recovery that the hospital would most likely not have available, nor would they be in the least bit interested in providing. Things like extra thick suture and PVC pipe for reconstruction; cloth ties for identifying and tagging vessels (a service to the embalmer who could then more easily isolate veins and arteries for formaldehyde injection); pint and quart-sized plastic containers like the ones at the grocery store salad bar; duct tape (the universal tool), and finally, the shroud, a plastic liquid-proof body-bag with a zipper.

The storage facility was within sight of my hotel. I pulled myself from the warmth of the bed and quickly threw on some clothes; I grabbed a cup of coffee and ventured through the lobby's automatic doors, out into the crisp night air. I could see my breath.

Then I saw Bert.

About a hundred yards from the hotel entrance and illuminated by the powerful storage unit spot lights, Bert was hastily dumping two large packages into the trunk of his badly dented 1972 lime-green Datsun coupe. I watched him climb behind the wheel next to a small crouching hooded figure in the passenger seat.

With two long cranks of the ignition, he fired up the engine and raced in my direction. The speed of Bert's actions reminded me that the team only had 24 hours from the time of the donor's final heart beat and consent to completing the recovery and icing down the tissue. Often, for a variety of reasons, there was a maddening delay between the time of death and obtaining consent. Apparently, we were down to the wire.

The Datsun screeched to a halt at the hotel's drive-through entrance. As Bert rolled down the window he smiled and said, "G*rrr*eg, our donor is waiting."

By this time I was excited, nervous, and apprehensive about the whole thing. I had taken bodies down to the morgue during my hospital transport orderly days, but this felt very different. What made things worse was getting the first sight of Jarred, Bert's scrub assistant—the other half of the two-man recovery team.

As I climbed in the back seat with my head touching the roof of the coupe, Bert quickly introduced Jarred, who turned to acknowledge me. Under the sweatshirt hood was a ghastly, disfigured face only a mother could love. Jarred had been in a fire when he was twelve. The entire left side of his face had a melted, stretched appearance. From outside the car, I could only see the right profile of his face. It was only when he turned that I got a close look at the dotted pock marks, the sticky scar creases that stretched as he turned toward me, the patch of pinkish-white skin and the runny eye that made me blink whenever I focused on it.

I couldn't help but wonder how nice it would feel right about now to be home in my own bed.

*　　*　　*

Bert was the lead cutter but Jarred was reputed to be just as efficient. Between the two of them a donor could be stripped of tissue in record time. We pulled out of the parking lot and immediately got on the freeway, heading to a small community hospital about 90 miles south. What little conversation arose came from Bert, who was difficult to understand in the first place. Jarred mostly nodded.

We turned into the hospital parking lot a little after 3:30 a.m., which meant Bert must have been averaging about 90 mph most of the trip. There was no way to know for sure, since the speedometer was one of many things broken in the vehicle.

The kits were quickly unloaded, as well as a large blue cooler with a long white handle and wheels. We made our way from the still black night into the florescent hospital and walked to the OR dressing rooms. The place was dead quiet and nearly empty.

Bert knew exactly where he was going. Surprisingly, the little rural hospital regularly called NTS for recoveries. I asked what was specifically known about our donor. Bert didn't have much information. Only that it was a 63 year-old white male who had died of an unspecified illness. Donor's name is Gadson... known to family and friends as Art.

Arthur Gadson! It was the husband of the woman whose voice I'd listened to at the call center. This was crazy. I told Bert and Jarred about the call, but neither was fazed. Bert said the nature of this business was inherently linked to pain, and our job was to provide a relief from some of that pain by bringing something good out of something bad. Sounded noble, but I still had to look Art in the eyes in a matter of minutes.

After a quick change into scrubs we headed to Room 2, where our donor awaited. He was lying on a stretcher with a thin sheet draping a formidable belly. Mrs. Gadson had consented to her husbands' bones, tendons, and skin. So we would be looking at a standard recovery time, hoping to be finished by 6:00 a.m.—just as the day shift would be arriving.

I didn't have to look Art in the eyes after all. They'd been removed.

The local eye bank staff had already claimed their prize—the corneas. Only the front surface of the eyeball was typically sliced off, rather than removal of the entire globe. Still, the procedure left its mark, and when Bert lifted the sheet to identify the body tag, Art lay naked with eyelids slightly parted. Like a trail of tears, thin lines of dried blood had crusted on each side of his face, coursing down from the outside corner of each eye, across the temples and curving around the tops of the ears. NTS wasn't the only company with a vested interested in Art.

Having correctly identified our donor, Bert and Jarred left the room to scrub at the sink in the center core of the OR while I waited in the room. I slowly approached the body and bent down to get a closer look.

Death is repulsively attractive. As I looked, thoughts began to fill my head. This is someone's father. This is someone's grandpa. This is a friend to many. This is Mrs. Gadson's lover. He looks a little like... at that point I had to look away.

The next thing I heard was the door being kicked open. I jumped a little as Bert snickered. After donning gowns, gloves, and masks, he and Jarred began draping the table that Art would be transferred to. Bert asked if I was sure I wanted to watch. Maybe he noticed the large circles of sweat under my armpits and wanted to be sure I wouldn't flip out. That would only delay things. I told him to go ahead. As the draping and transfer of the body was complete, Bert asked Jarred for the scalpel.

Before the incision he paused, turned toward me and said, "You need to know—this is bloody, it is messy, and isn't pretty. But it is necessary."

With that, Jarred noted the time from his position at the back table, which was covered with instruments including hammers, chisels, and a large hand held shaver known as a dermatome. This was used to remove the top layer of skin, which was then placed in plastic containers stacked on the corner of the table.

Bert began to slice with the passion and skill of a sushi master. He made full length incisions along the insides of the legs, and within minutes had removed three long bones from each leg—the tibia, fibula, and femur. Knee joints were separated and held aside. These would be placed in plastic containers for tendon extractions in the lab.

The hips were next. These were the trickiest, Bert had said. You could easily miss the 'sweet spot' at the joint allowing the cleanest separation, and mistakenly shatter the hip crest. Worse, if not careful, your hand could slip down the length of the chisel and be sliced open along with your donor.

The sections and pieces were passed to Jarred who deftly slipped each one into a bag, tied the top, and labeled with a marker pen. The two worked well together and anticipated each others' moves. Little talk was required.

It was time to flip Art over to take the dermas (skin). He was a big man, and it took all three of us to roll him over. Bert and Jarred were bear-hugging the torso and legs as I pulled the sheet up to help gain momentum. I wore rubber gloves but wasn't gowned, so I was careful not to contaminate anything. The squishy, wet sound and some deep grunts from us was all I heard as we got Art centered on the table face-down. The warm, coppery smell of open flesh filled my mask as the air wafted up. His entire back-side was dark purple from the pooled blood. The smell was familiar. But there was something different this time. There was an undertone—a blend of fermenting gas and feces. Decay was well underway.

Bert reached for the dermatome while Jarred located the nearest power outlet. Once the shaver was powered up, he made a couple of short test passes on the leg to adjust the blade's depth and thickness of the tissue. Satisfied with the samples, he began making long slow passes from the buttocks up to the shoulders as each strip of skin, like wet tissue paper, curled out the top. Bert carefully lifted each strip with metal tweezers called pick-ups, and dropped them into one of the solution-filled plastic cups Jarred had prepared at the back table.

Having liberated Art from everything consented for, it was time for reconstruction, which meant flipping him over.

Once we returned Art to the face-up or supine position, Bert roughly estimated the length of extremities and began cutting pieces of PVC pipe, which would serve as a makeshift skeleton. After the PVC was jammed into place, the surrounding muscle, fascia, and skin was stretched tightly around the pipe, while a continuous suture pattern called a 'mattress stitch' was used to close the long wounds from each ankle to the groin. Bert tagged the primary vessels needed for later embalming with cloth strips and left them dangling outside the sutured edges of the wound. The embalmer would appreciate this small detail.

* * *

It was just after 6:00 a.m. and Art was fully re-assembled. The cooler was packed with tissue and iced down, and Room 2 was left cleaner than when we arrived.

We dressed and made our way to the staff lounge in the hope that some sales rep would have donuts or muffins. We weren't disappointed. Grabbing our breakfast we headed out the front door with the remnants of Art, this time to a clear sunny day toward the Datsun, commonly referred to as the 'Donor-Mobile.' Here you might expect the story to end.

But it doesn't.

After the successful recovery, we had one small glitch. About halfway back to the NTS offices, Bert's 1972 lime-green Datsun decided to die—right on the Florida state highway.

Bert exploded with, "Aw sheet! I knew dis was coming!"

Right about then I could imagine the three of us standing next to the broken down rust-bucket with our thumbs sticking out; one with bad English, another with half a face, and the third holding a suspicious cooler. It was only 8:00 a.m., but the day seemed long already.

After calming down, Bert assured us there was no need to worry. It was a simple vapor lock in the engine. Happens all the time, he said. Once it cooled we would be on our way again. That's when I wanted to make sure we were going straight to the NTS office. Bert smiled and said, "Sorry man. We got to pick up my daughter and take her to school. Her mom is at work."

Within minutes, we pulled in the driveway of his house with Art patiently waiting in the trunk. The daughter, Danielle, climbed in the back seat with me and asked her daddy if he worked last night. Bert said that he had, and the little girl responded, "So it's in the trunk?" Bert nodded proudly, and off we drove to the local elementary school. Danielle seemed used to daddy's strange job and said nothing further during the ride. At the school's drop-off, she offered a quick hug, kiss, "Love you," and skipped off with her Dora the Explorer book bag bouncing as she joined her classmates.

Within a half hour we were back in the NTS parking lot. Bert took the cooler and headed for the processing area, Jarred found his car and started home, and I made my way through the offices for the obligatory 'goodbyes.' It was Friday morning. I had been up all night participating in one of the most gruesome experiences of my life. My only goal was to get through the office as quickly as possible, check out of the hotel, and go home.

*   *   *

Exhausted from the past eight hours, I walked down the center hall of NTS toward the main entrance where a cab was to be waiting. I passed several windows, looking only briefly into each.

The call center was humming as requesters counseled family members. The processing room technicians were opening coolers and sorting chunks of tissue. The tooling room lathe was spinning freshly cut segments, while in the adjoining room, the two futuristic Maytags cycled furiously and silently.

And The Dark Room—that lonely, mysterious holding area for the dead. Like the morgue in the basement of the

English church, the stacked remains were procured by way of fees, and their fate was questionable at best.

I walked by for the last time briefly stopping for a glance, but changed my mind and ignored it. Like everyone else. I reached the NTS lobby and pushed open the door.

Taking a deep, warm breath of the salty, moist air, I walked down the sidewalk and stepped off the curb where the cab driver waited. I reached for the handle, opened the door, and collapsed in the back seat.

Determination

—Chapter 13—

Homesick

"Health nuts are going to feel stupid someday,
Lying in hospitals dying of nothing."

Redd Foxx, Comedian

PERMISSION TO OBSERVE

The NTS job as a tissue procurement manager was insightful in many ways. I learned that in medicine, there needs to be balance, equity, and compassion. This holds true for any health-related profession. The drive for profitability must be fused with an equally passionate drive to promote survival, healing, and the best possible quality of life, which is probably why I was fired.

When the NTS board brought in a new CEO from one of the largest medical device manufacturers in the country to replace Patrick Graham, everything changed. The new leader immediately hired cronies from his old company and quickly assembled a team with the sole purpose of generating volume and profits to record levels, year after year. Unless you were deemed by the group to have come from the same mold, your services were no longer required.

Instructed to fly to Detroit for an informal territory strategy meeting with my new manager (one of the cronies), I arrived at the gate to be greeted by the new boss who was wearing an expensive black suit and stylish leather shoes. He looked ready for an interview. There was nothing informal about it.

With a limp handshake and a quick "How's it going?" it took all of 30 seconds to lose my job. My region was leading the country in growth and I had established lucrative contracts with several recovery agencies. I had also managed to salvage one particularly difficult agency which had threatened to work with a competitor once the news of the changing of the NTS guard was made public. The manager's parting message as he glanced at his watch was: "Hey good luck. I'm sure you'll find something."

Suddenly, I felt homesick. All I wanted to do was get on a plane and get back to St. Louis. I could feel my neck tense like a rope in a tug of war. Dizzy and nauseated, I barely made it to the restroom in time, only to dry heave. I hadn't eaten anything that morning and my head throbbed. So this, I thought, is how a successful career ends—barfing in an airport bathroom. By that time, unemployment was starting to look good.

*   *   *

The next four years was a time of waiting, thinking, and going broke. My six-figure income at a prestigious medical device manufacturer meant nothing now. Stripped of self-worth and desperate for income, I took a job as a Hall Monitor at a local high school. It's pretty sad when a role like that makes you feel like Barney Fife.

When I began the job I was issued two of the most powerful weapons an educator can have... a pad of Referral slips for writing up students, and a freshly charged walkie-talkie connecting me with the Administrators. Like Barney, all I really needed was a bullet in my breast pocket.

Despite my twisted gratification whenever I reached for my Referral pad and watched the sick look on the face of a busted student, I still felt like I was making a difference in a positive way. Sometimes the Hall Monitors were asked (directed is a better word) to substitute when a teacher was sick, or taking a much needed mental health day. The subbing included not only the horror of 50 straight minutes of confinement in a room full of hormone-raged teenagers; we were also expected to chauffeur large groups during field trip outings. Thank God I was never asked to accompany the marching band to the annual national competition. I can only imagine sitting on a bus for hours in front of the tuba section as they practiced Deep Purple's *Smoke on the Water*.

After two years, I was promoted to Library Assistant, working alongside two seasoned librarians. Arguably the cushiest job in the building—I was basically working for the health insurance coverage and had absolutely no money to spare. More often than not, lunch was a package of ramen noodles and some veggies at my desk. The result was a rapid depletion of the large 401K I had built from previous jobs.

The Library Assistant job included shelving books, helping teachers with audiovisual equipment, laminating posters, taking I.D. badge photos for new students, and patiently explaining (to unbelievably dense freshman) that the topic of 'cars' is *not* to be found in the encyclopedia's volume "C" but rather volume "A". You'd have to experience such a rudimentary intelligence level first-hand to fully appreciate the fact that it exists in today's youth. Hands down, it really does exist.

Yet the library role came with drawbacks. First and foremost was the pay. Health insurance premiums were eating up 50% of my income, but one of the other tough challenges was one that was intangible—*not* getting drawn into the daily gossip club. When three employees share a single office (and two of them are borderline man-haters), conversation routinely covered topics like how good men are at annoying their wives; the latest drama involving the other side of the family (usually deemed idiots); and how truly wonderful life is when husbands travel. I was more than ready for a new vocation.

My problem was that I was over fifty with a gnat-size income. I felt like a squirrel caught in a trap (absent nuts, of course).

I was about three years into my illustrious high school career when I had breakfast one Saturday morning with an old friend who, at the time, worked for one of the big St. Louis hospitals. He knew my history and suggested that I take some on-line refresher courses with the goal of returning to Respiratory Therapy. Going back to healthcare only made sense, he said.

Even after an absence of 33 years, I thought?

Age didn't matter, he insisted, and chances are there would always be some kind of meaningful work for me.

To be honest, during those three decades in corporate jobs, I missed that unique bond created when caring for the critically ill; the interaction and fulfillment is hard to duplicate in any other setting.

So I made some phone calls, looked into refresher classes, and once again plunged into the field of healthcare. For the first five months of 2011, I scoured medical journals, borrowed old respiratory textbooks from a friend (I had pitched all mine years before—convinced I would never again need them), and began an independent home study course designed to help new graduates pass the intense National Board exam.

One of the hurdles was that I had been away for so long that the rules had changed. The field of Respiratory Therapy in its infancy (formerly Inhalation Therapy) was as much on the job training as it was classroom based. Credentials were not required back then. You simply completed a two-year program and off to work you went. So I never bothered with National Boards. Today, candidates must complete multiple levels of testing, including an initial 4-hour Certification exam; and later conquer the more difficult 4-hour Registry exam. Finally, the dreaded comprehensive Clinical Simulation exam—a computer-based group of 10 patient scenarios in which you had to assess, diagnose, and treat each patient in a limited time, hopefully without killing one.

By mid-year 2011, I had passed the Certification exam, obtained my state license and one year later passed the remaining tests—all on the first attempt. That was huge. Even new graduates have difficulty passing everything on the first try. Here I was, out of the field for thirty years and able to return within six months. I knew then I was serious about my craft, and wanted a job where I could positively affect patient outcomes.

An opportunity presented itself quite by chance. In the summer of 2011, I began calling home care companies that provided respiratory care services and happened to stumble on an old work associate from Metropolitan. Alonso "Al" Pellegrini had worked the night shift at the Met the same time I worked days. Although our paths rarely crossed, we shared many of the same experiences and memories from the early days. I hadn't heard his name in over 35 years, but he remembered mine. Now he supervised one of the busiest respiratory home care services in the St. Louis area, and was looking for a therapist.

When we met the following week for an interview, we spent the first several minutes laughing about how some therapists never seem to leave the field (like us) and traded stories of old Met patients and employees. One involved the colorful antics of the Respiratory Therapy department Medical Director, Harrison E. Goldberg, M.D.

Harry Goldberg was a small, hunched man with thin wire-rimmed glasses and a thick, handlebar mustache. When walking behind him, his posture was reminiscent of a small bow-legged troll scurrying down a hillside to crouch under a bridge. As one of the primary pulmonary specialists and university faculty professors, Harry prided himself in his broad knowledge base and everyone else's stupidity.

In the old days many physicians and therapists smoked, which, unbelievably, was allowed anywhere in the hospital. It was not uncommon to see surgeons, visitors, even patients lighting up cigarettes. Surgeons would smoke between cases while others took a more fashionable approach, like puffing on a pipe during rounds.

Harry, on the other hand, took the privilege to new heights. The window sill of several MICU rooms (to this day) bare the burn trail of Marlboro cigarettes Harry would carefully perch just before inserting a three foot fiber optic scope down the throat and bronchial tubes of his patient. Harry was such a bad chain smoker that we called him the 'SS Goldberg' for the huge trail of smoke constantly wafting behind him.

One memorable story involved a famous confrontation between Harry and one of the more vocal nurses named June. Harry and June developed a reputation for mutual hatred and had countless public arguments over what constituted proper patient care. The battle-scarred relationship came to a head late on a Saturday afternoon.

At the end of a long shift, one of June's patients had unexpectedly arrested... just as Harry had begun a routine physical exam of the patient. June was outside the room and quickly responded to screams of, "Get me a nurse, we've got a code in here!" When June entered the room, she saw Harry frantically performing chest compressions as his glasses slid down his sweaty hawk nose; smoke trailing up from the cigarette on the window sill behind him.

When he looked up and saw it was June, Harry huffed commands with each compression, "I *said...* I *need...* a *real...* nurse!"

June, quick as ever, came back with something like, "Well I'm all you got right now!"

Harry, still huffing as June stood and watched, belted out, "*I... will have... your job... young lady!*"

June responded by pulling off her nurse's cap, flinging it in Harry's direction declaring, "Here you go... it's all yours."

By lunch time Monday, the story had circulated every corner of Metropolitan. Dirt and gossip travel at light speed in a hospital.

Some employees were betting on how quickly June would be canned, or if she would even be allowed to come back for her things. Before being placed on an immediate leave of absence until a formal decision was rendered, June had been summoned to meet with the Director of Nursing, Human Resource Manager, and the hospital Administrator.

By Thursday, word had leaked that a meekly written letter of apology had been sent. It arrived on Friday, and was opened with eager hands. The note, full of lament and regret over the lapse of personal professionalism and disrespect displayed during the confrontation, was signed;

"Yours Truly, Harrison E. Goldberg, M.D."

*   *   *

After trading a few more Metropolitan stories, Al described the home care therapists' job; setting up CPAP machines, managing patients on continuous ventilators, and training parents on the use of apnea monitors. It sounded like a pace that would be good for me, just coming back into the field. I would start by shadowing a therapist for a few weeks, getting the feel of the office environment, paperwork flow and learning how to best manage my time seeing patients. I would start the second week in July.

My trainer was a young therapist named Olive, a street-wise veteran of the home care market. Although quiet in my early ride-along trips, Olive gradually began to open up about her life and I soon realized she was not easily intimidated, nor did she harbor fond thoughts of the many welfare recipients we treated. She was clearly approaching burn-out.

One of those recipients happened to be my very first patient. After spending nearly three weeks together, Olive felt it was time for me to perform my first set-up. So we agreed that I would handle the entire visit from start to finish while Olive observed.

When we pulled up to the curb in front of our patient's tiny brick home, I noticed two things right away. The first was that the front door was posted with a sign that read: "No Smoking—Oxygen in Use". That was good. The other thing was that the front porch was cracked in large uneven sections and pulled several inches away from the foundation. Not so good.

After repeatedly pounding the door while standing in the July heat, we felt rhythmic vibrations in our feet as our patient approached the door. Upon arrival, the door cracked just enough for me to see the trail of smoke wafting up from the freshly-lit cigarette. It was the first sign of life.

The glowing white stick with ashes begging to be flicked, began bouncing rhythmically while the words were shouted, "Who is it!"

I thought of Eddy Murphy on *Saturday Night Live* when he showed how he answered the door in *his* neighborhood— Mister Rogers with an attitude.

Looking at Olive, I muttered, "Uh, Greg—from the respiratory therapy company 'mam. I'm here to set-up your CPAP machine. We had an appointment?"

As we stood on the crumbling porch, towering weeds filled the cracks along a crooked line of overgrown shrubs. Three badly stained dining room chairs had been lined up on the porch. The trio was positioned beneath the front picture window facing the street like a poor man's lawn set.

We heard a yell, "Gimme a minute!" as she waddled away from the door she'd left ajar. I'd like to think she had some idea of what she was expecting of us—to stand idle in exactly one hundred degrees in black scrubs with no shade.

We watched each others' neck sweat roll down into the scrub tops like little spitballs. The heat didn't bother Olive. Confident as a military officer, she had spent time earlier in her career as a security guard in a poor, South Chicago hospital. Few things on the street ever bothered her. Now, as a homecare Therapist, she could be as comfortable seeing patients in the worst housing projects as she was the classiest homes. I, however, did not share that same outlook.

The lucky patient that day was Loretta. She lived in a tiny ranch-style house in a clustered, run-down St. Louis neighborhood. It was well known that she had a serious weight problem complicating her sleep apnea condition. When she finally beckoned from her bedroom, we blindly crept through the dark, obstacle-laden living room. When we stepped into the bedroom, we gazed at our patient who easily tipped the scales at 450 pounds.

Propped on the edge of a king-size four post bed and desperately struggling to breathe sat Loretta. Like the world's largest Play-Doh lump, she was all mashed together in a pyramid blob wearing a tissue-thin gown printed with flowers and birds. She was surrounded by great billowing folds of dingy-white comforters, scraps of sticky notes, papers sliding out of manila folders, pill bottles (empty and full), oxygen equipment, bibles, snack bags, a used litter box and stack upon stack of unopened bills.

What captured my attention most was the size and shape of her hair. Naturally textured and roughly the diameter of a beach ball, the globe surrounding Loretta's head was perfectly round and dark as a mossy forest.

As I fumbled to set up the CPAP machine and began explaining the operation of the unit, it occurred to me that I faced the daunting task of positioning the headgear straps and face mask. "You sure have a lot of hair," I offered as I wiped more sweat from my forehead.

Taking a deep breath I raised the straps, stretching them like bungee cords—and snapped them over the giant bouffant. Fortunately, Loretta seemed to be taking things in stride. I finally got the straps detangled from the monster-do without ripping out too many strands. I was then able to seat the mask over her nose and mouth, and once the machine was turned on, she seemed relieved and pleased that the pressure was comfortable.

"Ooh Lordy," came a muffled coo from inside the mask, "That's good."

Olive took note of my every move and appeared satisfied with the progress of the visit.

Following the instructions for care of the equipment, I took off the headgear, clumsily dropping one of the two plastic clips used to secure the straps to the mask. Frustrated, I said, "Well, I guess I lost the clip. It's down here somewhere." With that, the three of us began our search. It had to be wedged in the folds of the bed comforter—otherwise we would have heard a 'click' as it hit the wood floor.

I knelt down to look under the bed just to be sure, while Olive scanned the room from her vantage point next to the bedroom window. As Loretta rummaged through the folds of her sheets, she suddenly shrieked, "Well looky here!" Delighted at discovering a small pile of old potato chip fragments, she deftly scooped up the bunch, devouring them in a single gulp.

I feared the worst. The visit was sure to be a bust, since the mask was useless without both clips. How would she be able to start her CPAP therapy? I looked to my trainer who calmly stated that we could drop some off later in the day. There was no need to fret. In a rush of relief, I turned toward Loretta to gauge her response.

That was when I saw it.

I spied the long lost clip—buried deep in a thicket of hair. "Wait a minute. I think I see it!" I exclaimed. "Hold still." I was tempted to dramatically roll up the sleeve of my scrub and declare, "I'm going in!" But I held back. It was enough just to find the darned thing and complete the appointment on a positive note.

Having retrieved the orphaned clip and threaded the strap through the slot (making sure to squeeze the Velcro fasteners *extra* tight), I placed the mask and harness inside the cloth draw-string pouch we supplied with the set-up.

Picking up my clipboard with the paperwork to be signed, I noticed movement out of the corner of my eye. It wasn't Olive. Something had buzzed my head, and slowly descended to the comforter. Landing like a drone midway between Loretta's bare leg and my cat-hair coated scrubs was a robust, inch-long yellow jacket. We all saw it at the same time.

159

"Lord God Almighty!" screamed Loretta, "Oh Jesus!" She began to pant, "Kill it! I'm allergic to them things and if it stings me I will be right back in that hospital—swellin' up and fixin' to die! Have mercy!"

With no time to take off my shoe and give the critter a good swat, all I could think of was to slam something on it. With both hands gripping the clipboard, I raised it above my head and buried it in the cover folds, smashing the wasp.

I waited a few seconds until I thought it was safe. As I slowly lifted the board I could see that the beast was only stunned, and more determined to attack than ever. Quickly slamming the clipboard once more, I said as calmly as I could, "I need a paper towel or tissue to grunch him up."

With none in sight, Loretta grabbed an unopened envelope from one of the mountains of bills on her dresser. "Here... use this! I ain't a gonna' be payin' that one no way," she said confidently.

Making the switch from clipboard to envelope in a single swoop, I quickly pinched the wasp, relieved to hear the distinctive 'pop.'

Coughing from all the excitement and laboring to catch her breath, Loretta thanked us repeatedly between gasps. After a while she settled down enough for us to finish the paperwork and be on our way.

*   *   *

We left Loretta's house that steamy summer day having learned some valuable lessons. First; always maintain control of the situation, especially when the unexpected occurs. Second; remain calm and reassuring to the patient at all times. Third, if a mask clip is ever misplaced at the time of set-up, pray it doesn't end up in a pile of broken potato chips.

And finally, it might not hurt to carry a can of wasp spray in the car.

—Chapter 14—

Pet

"I poured spot remover on my dog.
Now he's gone."

Steven Wright, Comedian

PERMISSION TO OBSERVE

Some might look at it as a job perk; others, a privilege. As far as I'm concerned, I would avoid all pets for the remainder of my career if at all possible.

A dog is one thing, but sharing living space with an exotic animal or wild beast is a flawed lifestyle at best. What's worse is when the living space is confined, like that of a mobile home.

One of the more memorable trailer parks I visited as a homecare therapist had a large deck at the entrance of one of the many colorful double-wide trailers. Three of the four steps leading up to the door of this particular dwelling were either missing or broken.

Arranged on the floor of the deck was what amounted to a small general store. It was complete with not one but *two* blue toilets perched side-by-side (one apparently functional); three beat-up oxygen concentrators; a partially-assembled Harley Davidson; a pet cage with something moving but unidentifiable curled up inside; various art and craft supplies all ruined by weather, and a rotting office desk with a cash register on top. The drawer was open and empty of change, but something had built a nest in the $20 bill section.

No matter who (or what) waited as you stepped inside a mobile home, you could almost always count on seeing the largest and most expensive flat-screen televisions. Invariably, the volume would be blaring with either the theme music from a Law & Order episode, or Judge Judy berating a litigant in a ridiculous civil case. There seems to be a prevailing interest in TV programming of a legal nature. However, lest I unfairly stereotype our government-dependent friends, I will share my story of Maggie.

* * *

I was filling in for one of our vacationing therapists who covered the rural central Missouri territory, a popular tourist area well known for award-winning wines and beautiful, sprawling vineyards. The medical history of my first scheduled patient that week involved a woman in her early

162

60's who was recuperating from back surgery and having difficulty with her leaking CPAP mask. My task was to fix the leak or give her a new mask.

The home she shared with her husband and Maggie was an expensive custom ranch, perched on the side of a manicured grassy hill with a backdrop of thick forest and view of one of the local vineyards. The walkway from the pebble stone wrap-around driveway sparkled in the morning sun and was lined with a colorful array of flowers, shrubs and edge stones. It was a peaceful, picturesque scene worthy of a greeting card.

Savoring the sights and smells of the moment, I strolled toward the stained-glass entrance of the grand foyer and paused to take a deep breath. Thankful that not every visit consisted of trailer parks, widescreen televisions, and that unmistakable triad of aromas—nicotine, vegetable oil, and cat urine, I rang the bell. That simple act set things in motion.

Like the starter's gun in a race, immediately a series of screams and screeches came from inside the house and penetrated both the door and my eardrums. What came to mind later was the shower scene in *Psycho* where Anthony Perkins plunges the knife over and over into Janet Lee and you hear those horrible, piercing shrieks.

I jumped back a step, but still made an attempt to peek through the side glass pane to see who was being murdered. Seconds later, a shadowy figure reached for the knob.

As the door began to swing open, an overly-comforting voice said, "Maggie, Maggie Dear, it's alright. We have a visitor."

Erect as a drill sergeant stood Mrs. Helen Landau, a tall woman with beady, half-opened eyes and straight black hair that reached down her lower back nearly brushing the back of her knees. Because of the surgery (and the fact she was wearing a brace), she was forced to shuffle rather than step aside for me to enter. With the endless black hair and her sleepy-eyed look, she bore an uncanny resemblance to Morticia from *The Addams Family*.

The scene unfolding before me in the living room was dreamlike. Every piece of furniture including floor lamps, tables, piano, and television was completely draped in sheets, blankets, or towels. Full sections of newspaper covered every inch of carpet as far as I could see, which wasn't all that far because my attention quickly shifted to the family pet.

Standing on the back of the sofa facing me with wings spread wide was Maggie the crow. I felt like I was in a giant, luxurious bird cage... eye-to-eye with the occupant.

Her wingspan nearly matched the length of the sofa. Maggie's black marble eyes glared while she craned her neck, darting a thick red tongue in my direction. I was probably three feet from this highly agitated of God's creatures. While she cawed madly, I heard a series of loud pops. I realized the sound was coming from her talons, which, one by one, poked through the sofa back, giving her plenty of traction in the event Helen gave the command to gouge my eyes out like the school teacher in *The Birds*.

Helen seemed to be in her own world as Maggie became more aggressive. No doubt wigged-out on narcotics from the surgery, she stood stiffly with her head slightly tilted. She watched with glazed, half-opened eyes and finally spoke to the bird; "It's alright Maggie Dear. He's a friend. He won't hurt Mommy."

Immediately the bird calmed. Never having encountered a scene like this, it took me a minute to regroup and finally ask the question, "I understand you are having some problems with your mask, Mrs. Landau?"

Her eyes widened as she replied, "You may call me Helen. This way please."

As she slowly turned to lead me down the hall to her bedroom, Maggie leaped off the sofa and began walking behind me. Actually, her gait was more of a waddling lope as she squawked along the way. I looked over my shoulder to make sure I wasn't about to get my ankles pecked and watched as she shifted her weight from side-to-side with each step, determined to keep pace. I wondered if her wings had been clipped to hold her captive in the Landau house, which now served as the family aviary.

Before reaching the master bedroom we passed the dining room where an artificial Christmas tree stood tall in one corner. This wouldn't have been unusual except for the fact that it was the middle of summer and seemed strangely inappropriate. The tree was draped in large, gaudy, unlit lights, while the only ornaments remaining were randomly placed bits of aluminum foil. Not known for my shyness in home settings, I asked why the holiday tree was still up. She was happy for the chance to explain by telling me that the tree serves as one of Maggie's many amusements, and proceeded to demonstrate.

The crow loved to retrieve pieces of foil stashed in various nooks around the house. Helen's husband, Gerald, a brilliant electrical engineer by day, devoted much of his time doting on the bird and concealing scraps of Reynolds Wrap. Upon discovery and retrieval of foil, Maggie would cackle and lope toward the tree with her prize clamped tightly in her beak.

As Helen met the crow to accept the foil and decorate yet another empty space on the tree, she carefully tucked it in place speaking the words Maggie had been patiently awaiting: "Ok Maggie, sparkle time!"

The bird then flapped its wings and let out a single screech while standing directly beneath the lowest limb. Immediately, the tree's lights blazed, and the bits of foil twinkled as Maggie squawked in delight.

Gerald, it turns out, used his keen engineering prowess to rig up a 'Clapper' switch on the bottom of the tree. This gave the stupid bird control of the lights. Had I not seen it, I wouldn't have believed it. "Exactly how smart is this bird?" I asked.

Helen replied, "Oh, very bright indeed. We've even taught her to speak." She then turned toward the crow and began coaxing by saying, "I love you Maggie, I love you!" several times.

Maggie cocked her head and cawed something raspy like, "rah ruv rue!"

Having ended the demonstration, Helen led the way to the bedroom. I followed her to the side of the bed where the CPAP machine and mask were connected. Ever so slowly she backed up and gradually lowered herself to a sitting position on the edge of the bed. The back pain must have been intense. Waiting for her to settle, I turned to see my newest friend hopping across the threshold like a carefree inquisitive child.

"Mrs. Landau, we'll need to apply your mask as if you were going to bed so we can check the whole system for leaks. But I have to tell you, I'm a little concerned that Maggie might not appreciate me getting near your face. Will she freak out?"

She paused and said, "Certainly not sir. I have complete control of her. She minds me like a child. Actually, she *is* our child."

Helen did seem to have control. Maggie just stood and watched as I gently strapped on the mask and checked all the connections. The solution ended up being pretty simple. The mask was shot and she needed a replacement.

Afterward, we engaged in a little small talk as I packed up my samples and had her sign papers. I asked how Maggie responded to 'Daddy' Gerald.

"Oh yes," she offered, "They get along marvelously. They have a special game they play every evening before supper."

As we made our way back to the foyer, Maggie gave a couple of mighty flaps and once again perched herself on the sofa—right where she was when I arrived. Helen went on to explain the game:

"Every afternoon when Gerald gets home from work, we all retire to the bedroom for a 30 minute nap. Gerald and I relax in the queen size bed with our CPAP machines on while Maggie hops on the corner chair beneath the window. Once the nap is complete, I wake up first and let the other two know that I am heading to the kitchen to start the evening meal. That is Gerald's signal to begin the game.

"He takes off his mask and hangs it on the bedpost. Then he turns and begins slinking toward Maggie using a teasing, sing-song voice while showing her his tightly clenched fist, '*Maggie* girl... look what *Daddy* has for you... a special *treat!*' He then makes his way over and stands next to her chair as she anxiously awaits her prize, only to watch him slowly open his fist one finger at a time, until the palm is spread wide... and empty."

Mrs. Landau chuckled as she continued telling the story.

"Then, Maggie squawks and pecks Gerald's palm as punishment for the tease. Gerald grabs his 'injured' hand and yelps in pain as he runs frantically in circles. Maggie finds it most amusing."

As she spoke, her chuckles became faster and louder. Soon she was hysterical - roaring with laughter as she desperately tried to catch her breath:

"Then," she chuckled, "like lifelong pals, they leave the room together and head for the kitchen, barely able to contain themselves from the laughter."

After a moment and several breaths, she collected herself, paused to take one last deep breath, and lovingly smiled at Maggie saying, "But it's a wonderful way to start the evening, isn't it dear?"

—Chapter 15—

The Collection

"Zoo:
An excellent place to study the habits of
humans"

Evan Esar, American Humorist

GREGORY R. FROST, RRT

People collect fascinating things. Most of us are, or have been collectors of something. Be it bottle caps, comic books, baseball cards, or Barbie dolls—there are some things that will always hold a special place in the heart.

My interest as a teen, however, leaned more toward the gruesome. I loved horror movies. Willing to spend my entire allowance in a heartbeat, I bought whatever I could put my hands on that might offer shock value to impress friends and family members.

A devoted fan and avid collector of the magazine *Famous Monsters of Filmland*, I used to ride my bike every week to Abel Drug at the edge of the Jennings city limit so I could check the shelves for the latest copy. It was less than a mile from my house, but felt like a country away.

Tuesday is when all the new magazines came in. I can still remember some of the cover images; Creature from the Black Lagoon, Dracula, Wolf Man, Frankenstein, and Rodan—the awkwardly flying Japanese monster. The magazines managed to keep me penniless for years.

Even as a young adult with three children, I held on to this strange fascination for the unusual. Several years ago, I owned a basketball-size clear glass globe mounted on a wooden stand. The ball contained a real octopus, complete with slick, beige colored tentacles that stuck to the inside wall of the glass. It served as a wonderful conversation piece in the family room. After a few years the liquid preservative began to cloud, and it was becoming difficult to see 'Ollie'.

I remembered that my then neighbor across the street was a licensed funeral director, and had access to certain items of interest, formaldehyde being one. Often chatty and proud of his particular line of work, Ralph Bishop and I frequently met at the curb while watering our lawns or picking weeds and talked shop. He would enjoy showing off the latest tools of the trade and was always bringing unusual items home.

Things like the latest design in bone dissectors or an improved high-speed autopsy saw (which doubled as a baseboard trimmer) were always available for Ralph to demonstrate and expound upon. Probably the one that I found troubling was a small hand-held gadget he kept in his left front pocket. The thing had a handle with an attached blade of sorts, with a blunt 90 degree curve at the tip. It was called an 'aneurism hook'. I never asked what he used it for at home.

It always fascinated me as I talked with Ralph at the curb and learned all about his unique profession, except for the fact that he was fall-down drunk nearly every night. I suppose the daily work routine involving death was stressful. Or maybe it had to do with the fact that his boss, Lawrence Brampton (owner and founder of Brampton's Funeral Home) lived directly across the street from Ralph and could observe his movement... not just during the day, but during the evening, every evening, and all weekend.

On week nights, whenever Ralph emerged from his house in early evening to stand with the garden hose in hand (usually flooding a single spot), and a cocktail in the other, I knew he was deep in thought. If his mind wasn't occupied by the latest body he was working on, he would worry that Brampton was spying from his living room with a pair of binoculars. Ralph suffered from paranoia as well as mild depression.

One day I got the idea to ask if he could maybe scrounge some chemicals for me so I could give Ollie a much needed bath and refill the globe with fresh formaldehyde. If Ralph was a collector of embalming instruments, I figured there was a pretty good chance he'd be able to spot me for a little controlled substance... especially if he was drunk when I asked.

One evening, I carried Ollie across the street where Ralph was intently focused on a patch of grass (now mud), teetering ever-so-slightly as he stood.

"Take a look at this Ralph," I said as he turned to spy the thing in the glass.

His eyes became like globes themselves and he slurred, "Whatha hell *is* that?"

"Ralph," I replied, "This is actually a fifty year old rare species of octopus that was caught somewhere in the Gulf of Mexico, probably worth a whole lot of dough." I continued to embellish, "We don't know who caught it, or for that matter, how my wife's grandfather ever got hold of it. He had a way of procuring weird stuff. But what I *do* know is that it's in dire need of cleaning, and I don't know where I can get a good grade of formaldehyde without going through a lot of Material Safety Data hassles. Think you can help?"

Ralph thought for a moment as he looked up toward Brampton's house, each eyelid blinking at different times. With difficulty forming words he said, "Man, I could get in shome deepshit for something like that!"

"Brampton doesn't have to know," I replied. "Think of it like this. I'm going to donate this thing to the local elementary school science department anyway. I just need to clean it up. You'd be furthering the education of young, impressionable minds and *you*, Ralph, might just inspire one of those young people to grow up and become a professional embalmer. Literally, you could be the hero."

The alcohol was working. I could see it in his eyes (one at a time). At the prospect of immediately becoming a positive role model, Ralph eagerly agreed to provide me with a batch of body juice from the funeral home. Giving a nod of his head for me to lean closer, he began a slurred whisper of instructions and demands.

"You got to promise you won't tell Brampton 'bout this—even if he ashks you. I could get fa...fired for it!"

"Ralph," I assured him, "It won't go any further."

PERMISSION TO OBSERVE

*   *   *

The next evening, I waited from my single step porch at the pre-determined time and watched as Ralph peeked out his screen door, looking from left to right like a kid getting ready to jay-walk an intersection. Then, he stared directly at Brampton's picture window, making sure the coast was clear.

Attempting to make a straight bee-line but failing miserably, Ralph walked a zigzag path as he cradled the gallon jug of formaldehyde like a football. He ducked behind the huge sweet gum tree trunk in the center of my front yard, poised for a hand-off.

Dizzy and out of breath, he handed me the glass jug and whispered, "Here you go. And remember, *not a word*!"

I looked at the chemical which, unexpectedly, contained a few bits of debris floating on the surface. Not feeling I should complain at this point, or worse, ask if the stuff was fresh or recycled, I decided to let it go.

He then turned and made a valiant effort to take a casual stroll back to his front door with one hand in his pocket, but that only served to throw him off balance and ended up weaving the same path he came. As he stepped in the doorway, he took one last look toward Brampton's house, offered a little backward salute in my direction and stumbled inside.

I don't think Brampton ever caught on, which is good because I could have been slammed with a hefty fine for contaminating the environment with the spent formaldehyde from Ollie's globe. The good news is that the globe was delivered to the science department with crystal clear fluid bathing Ollie's tentacles.

Who knows, maybe down the road when the embalmer works on me, he will have been inspired by a grade school octopus in a globe. Some legacy.

*   *   *

When I asked a few homecare colleagues if they had seen any unusual collections in their careers, one manager, Terri, offered her story of her eighteen year-old son, Nick, who has been diagnosed with severe autism. At the time of the incident, Nick was fifteen and ready, mom thought, to be taking care of his own needs during the day while she worked. Having made every possible preparation to make the house safe, she let Nick know that she would be calling regularly throughout the day, and left for work.

All was quiet that first day, Terri having called Nick on the hour, every hour. Each time she called, he assured her that he was fine and all was well. The only thing he mentioned was that he had started a new collection he was proud of and that he would show her as soon as she got home.

The house looked exactly the same when she returned that evening and so did Nick, except for the crudely-etched tattoo he had printed along the entire length of his leg. Using a straight pin and bottle of India ink he'd found in the kitchen junk drawer, he had scribbled the phrase:

I ♡ MOM

Turns out Nick had decided to start an art collection on his body.

He informed Terri that he planned to cover every square inch of his skin with cool shapes by the time he turned eighteen. He even had time to do a second tattoo, this time on his upper left arm that read:

I Like Nachos

* * *

Not long ago, my work load had reached an all time high, with patient appointments scheduled back-to-back nearly every day. On a frigid Tuesday afternoon at 5:30 in mid-January, it was already depressingly dark, and I was late, cold, and lost.

I was seriously considering turning back and chucking this one. The scheduler at the office had allowed extra time to get to the house since it was tucked deep in the woods and the chance of my GPS picking up the address was slim to none. To top it off, cell phone service was non-existent, having tried several times to call someone at the residence for directions.

The patient, Claire Brown, was in her late sixties and suffered from severe COPD. A forty plus year smoker, she was, for the most part, tethered to her continuous oxygen and used a CPAP machine to help her sleep. She was recently discharged from the hospital for a bad bout with pneumonia. I was instructed to make a follow up visit and provide new supplies and re-instruction if needed.

As I drove slowly along the pitch black road, I shivered from the window being down in the hope of getting a better view of the tiny, gold address stickers on the sides of the rusty mail boxes. Worse was trying to decipher barely-legible paint-brushed numbers along the post. The mailboxes that I did see were few and far between.

Frustrated and freezing, I decided to give up and let the office know I couldn't locate *29007 Highway OO*, and that they would need to reschedule the visit—preferably during the light of day. Turning around in the next available driveway, my headlight beams produced a number on the side of a box, '*29007*'. I had to slam the brakes as soon as I'd centered the car in the gravel drive since it was blocked by an enormous cattle gate upon which hung several signs. All of them warnings; "No Trespassing"; "Beware of Dog"; "Attack Dogs"; "Caution"; and "No Hunters Allowed."

My cell phone rang and I jumped. Great, *now* I get cell service. Fumbling for the phone's flip piece I opened it and answered, "This is Greg."

GREGORY R. FROST, RRT

The caller's voice was thick and slow, like south Alabama slow. He sounded like Junior Samples from *Hee Haw*—about to beg me to call *BR-549* whenever I need a fine used car. "Uh, this here's Bobbie, though most people call me 'Red', an' ah think yuse here for mah wife, Claire."

"Yes I am," I said. "Had a hard time finding you Red Brown."

He thought a moment and I could tell he grinned, "Thas' just the way we like it."

Having stepped out of the car warily approaching the gate, I could see that Red was standing at the open door under his porch light about a hundred yards off, holding the phone against an ear. There was enough light from my beams to see that the gravel road took a deep dip toward a dry creek bed and continued sharply up a steep hill to the house.

There was something else. Vaguely familiar vocalizations and grunts coming from the surrounding woods—bays, howls, hoots and screeches that sounded like background jungle noise in a National Geographic special.

Turning my attention back to the phone, I listened to Red continue slowly as I stood at the gate wishing he would talk faster, "Ah' ken sees yoo from here. All yoo need to do is lift up that there war latch, swing the big gate open, and come on thoo."

Of course my immediate response was, "Red, what about the dogs?"

"Ain't got no dogs!" he replied. "Them signs jus' to keep the damn neighbors out. Ah ken ashure you, ah got evuhthin'else in here trained. And by thuh way," he continued, "Jus make sure yoo block that gate when yoo open it up, 'cause it'll slam hard on the side of yo' car. Me an' Shadow here'll be a waitin'."

No dogs? Everything is *trained*? Who is *Shadow*?

I opened the gate as instructed, propping it with a log that was conveniently placed along the gravel edge. Careful

175

to close it after inching forward enough to clear the gate's swing, I climbed back in the cold car and proceeded down the grade and up the hill, cresting at a point just short of the main driveway.

That's when my headlights lit up the backside of Red who, at the moment, was positioned at a 45 degree angle to the ground in spread-eagle fashion, with both arms locked in a heated struggle with the horns of an unidentified beast.

With his back toward me, he looked like a leaning sumo wrestler dressed in overalls, desperately trying to hold back the opponent. The beast was pushing Red hard enough to cause his feet to slide atop the gravel surface. The pair of horns was sizeable and Red used them as handles to try to steer the creature.

I put the transmission in park but kept the engine running, in case *I* needed to run. Red looked over his shoulder and motioned with his head for me to go to the front door. "Claire's in thire," he breathlessly puffed, " Go 'head in. She's awaitin for ya in the livin' room. I'll hold Shadow here 'til yoos inside."

Pausing for a breathe he continued, "He jes' playful and nosey, thas all. Damn things' too dumb to know any better. He's libel to charge right into the front a yo' car iffin I don't stop 'im. 'Bout as smart as a damned guppy prob'ly."

Shadow was a goat. The largest goat I had ever seen. He looked more like a cross between a goat and a Clydesdale, if such a thing were possible—with long, sharp horns and strength to match. I later learned from Red that Shadow was actually a Spanish goat or 'scrub goat', prized for its ability to supply milk, meat, hair, and in the 1900's, Angora fur.

More important to ranchers in Texas, though, was the fact that the Spanish goat could be used to clear vast acreage of brush, in particular, a beautiful little yellow flower with heart-shaped petals known as the Bitterweed. The weed, poisonous and lethal to sheep and cattle, is apparently considered a delicacy by the goats.

*   *   *

As the headlights of my car dimmed, there was still enough light cast from the porch to see that Shadow had suddenly lost interest in me, having spotted a random cluster of weeds popping up through the driveway gravel. He dropped his head and began foraging. Realizing it was safe, Red brushed off his overalls and led me to the steps. "We ok now. His stomach done took over his brain."

Before stepping onto the porch, I caught a glimpse of two sets of greenish-gold eyes to my left, glowing in the light and following my every move. As they were drawn closer, I could see it was a pair of smaller (by comparison) rams, badly in need of shearing, and wafting up a hot musky stench that cut through the night air.

With fully curled horns, the rams were covered in grey wool that was matted, badly tangled and littered with bits of leaves, twigs and fuzz. The wool hung so low under their bellies that it moved back and forth as they walked, brushing the ground and swaying like long felt strips in a car wash.

More striking than their appearance was their behavior. They moved in complete unison, like a team of synchronized swimmers. Left, right, starting, stopping, and backing up. No matter the action they were together. Never separated by more than a few inches, and never getting closer to a human than about ten feet.

As we walked into the house, I asked Red about them. He said that they had been "wethered" seven years ago, which, translated in Red's terms is... "Ah cut they nuts off," he boasted. "They's been skittish ever since. Won't let nobody get close to 'em. Guess I would be too iffin' mine was a cut off."

I asked what he could possibly do with the rams since they couldn't be used for wool.

He replied, " 'Bout all they's good fer is eatin' grass. I ain't had to mow for seven years. Saves a lot on gas."

By this time my lips were getting numb and Red could see I was shivering, so we made our way through the front door, stepping just inside the living room. Still wearing the glasses I normally use for night driving, my lenses fogged from the sudden temperature change. But before doing so, I saw Claire sitting in her rocker with her nasal oxygen tucked tightly in place, slowly rocking something in her lap that had large beady eyes and a rat-like tail. It resembled a possum.

Stopping dead in my tracks, I lowered my chin to be able to see over the top of the fogged glasses and wondered how bizarre this visit could get—and if I needed to just turn around and leave. But then I'd have to get past Shadow again.

With a nervous chuckle, I greeted Claire and immediately asked what the thing was on her lap, and more important, if it had a problem with strangers.

Claire was constantly short of breath and was forced to speak in broken sentences. "This," she said, "is... a Sphynx... a hairless... cat... from Canada". "We... named... him 'Smeagol'... after... the... *Lord of... The Rings*... character."

Letting his wife catch her breath, Red went on to explain that the cat is very affectionate and likes attention. Once able to see through my glasses, I approached Claire and reached out to offer Smeagol a quick pet. I was more curious to see what the skin felt like than to try to become friends with something that looked more like a troll than a cat.

Expecting a cold, sticky sensation when I ran my hand over the deep wrinkles, I was surprised by the opposite. Touching the skin was like feeling an overly-ripened, hot peach. The unusual warmth made it feel like the cat had a fever. According to *Animal Planet*, the breed's metabolism runs higher than most, causing about four degrees difference in temperature. Petting the little creature was most unpleasant.

As Claire let Smeagol slip from her lap, I made the mistake of asking how a cat like that manages to amuse himself. Red pointed toward the corner of the dining room where two duck-like animals huddled together and immediately began honking when Smeagol was released.

"Them's Chinese Geese," Red offered. "They's real good watchdogs. Bleached white with bright orange feet and bills that supported large orange fleshy knobs, the geese were clearly anxious—honking and flapping nervously in small circles as Smeagol slowly approached.

Claire continued to rock and forced a smile as she struggled to breathe. Red, on the other hand, seemed to enjoy the stalking of the geese by his beloved cat and watched in silence. Finally Claire huffed, "Red!... you'd better... let them two... out... It's been a while... since they crapped. They been... over there... nibblin'... on Smeagol's litter..."

Reluctantly, Red moved between the geese and their would-be attacker, shooing them toward the door as they waddled out as fast as their legs would carry them. "He wouldn't of hurt 'em Claire. He jes likes to bat at them orange balls they got stuck on they heads."

Sensing that all the performances had finally ended, at least for the moment, I took the opportunity to review the CPAP machine with Claire and answer her many, breathless questions.

After about twenty minutes, I was satisfied with her (and Red's) understanding of the equipment and asked if they needed anything else. Content to call it a night, we completed the necessary paperwork. They seemed genuinely relieved, thanking me several times as I gathered my things together.

Red walked toward the door as he looked my way, "Yude better gimme a head start so's I can corral Shadow. Dumb as he is, he no doubt forgot yoo's even here. Might try to come at yoo agin."

Glad to comply, I watched through the storm door's glass panel, giving Red as much time as he needed to resume his Sumo stance with Shadow.

Having firmed his position, he nodded for me to come out, and I quickly made my way back to the car. Before stepping in, I stopped to ask Red what Shadow normally ate, since they'd raised him from a kid.

"Pretty much whatever he can find," replied Red. "He does have his favorites though; he's particlarly fond of only two things.That'd be poison ivy... and oatmeal cookies."

Wrestling with the sharp set of horns and quickly getting winded he said, "Damned if he don't jes' gulp down a whole dozen at a time—paper plate and all. Claire cooks up a batch once and a while, but I think the idiot is plane spoilt. He hangs around the back porch by the kitchen, like he's homeless or somethin', always lookin' for a handout." Pausing to breathe, Red thanked me one more time and bid me a good day, which, thankfully, was over.

*   *   *

I made my way to the car, which by this time was thoroughly refrigerated. I started the little four cylinder engine as it wheezed and choked to life. I immediately cranked up the noisy heater blower.

Rubbing my hands together for warmth, I steered with my elbows and headed back down the hill, stopping to open the gate. This time though, after pulling off the property and closing the gate I settled into my seat and turned the blower to the 'off' position.

Lowering the window all the way before shifting the car in gear, I heard the sound of the Brown's collection in the distance coming to life: Chinese Geese honking, rams and goats baying, squeals from pigs I couldn't see, and over it all—the faint voice of Red cursing up a storm. I could only guess that Shadow nipped his arm or stomped one of his feet as he looked for more fresh weeds.

I pulled onto the blacktop road from the gravel drive as the cries of the night served as my benediction. The noises gradually faded. I shivered as I rolled up my window, turned up the heater, and headed home.

Priceless

"The value of experience is not in seeing much,
But in seeing wisely"

William Osler, M.D.

GREGORY R. FROST, RRT

As I write this sitting at my office desk, positioned on one of the bookshelves lining the walls is a very small, very old hand-blown flask. Standing less than five inches high and only half an inch in diameter, the glass jar resembles a laboratory test tube or small beaker. It is slightly fluted around the top edge and bowled at its base so that it can hold liquid. Mounted and encased in a protective dome, the flask dates back to the Roman period—somewhere between 63 B.C. and 330 C.E.

The Israeli Department of Antiquities has verified the object, which carries its own Certificate of Authenticity #1340 from the Old City of Jerusalem, Via Dolorosa no.33.

It is called a *lachrymatory*—a tear bottle—used during the biblical era by professional (paid) mourners to collect the shed tears of those attending a wake, and would later be placed alongside the dead as a burial offering and sign of respect:

"You number my wanderings; Put my tears into Your bottle. Are they not in Your book? Psalm 56:8.

As I run my fingers slowly down the neck of the smooth bottle, tilting it to peer deep inside, I see the dark, dried particles resting on the bottom and can't help but wonder who may have originally crafted the jar and what was going through his mind when the glass was shaped.

More interesting, though, is the question of purpose... whose tears were actually collected, and who was being wept for? I suppose it could have been anyone, yet it would seem obvious that the poor would not have been able to afford mourners. Therefore it must have been someone of means.

Maybe the tears came from an individual who'd had a remote encounter with Jesus at some point. The dating certainly fits. Or maybe they came from one of his many followers... or one of his enemies. Jesus himself wept at the funeral of his beloved Lazarus. Perhaps His tears were saved in the jar I hold.

I suppose you could categorize tears as one of the more unusual 'collections' I have touched on. I once knew a young minister who became Pastor of our local church. He had a nasty habit of nervously chewing and clipping his fingernails. Worse, he would collect the remnants in the top drawer of his desk at the church. Whenever he counseled members he would fling (or spit) each shred into the open drawer, while staring at the member seated across from him. I can't begin to explain behavior like that.

What I *can* explain is this. I've come to a point in my life where I no longer collect things. No more treasured monster magazines, or ghastly bloated cephalopod specimens, or college brochures, or, for that matter, tears. Collecting material 'stuff' doesn't hold the same appeal it once did.

So what is fundamentally important? Author Richard J. Leider in his book *The Power of Purpose* says, "Every one of us, somehow, wants to leave footprints. Purpose is unique to each of us, alone. We must each discover our own."

What exactly is it that motivates me in this strange work setting I have chosen? What do I seek, and cling to? I've thought about it a long time, and it's not easy to explain.

I think the best answer is *knowledge*. Not the scholarly type or the level of intelligence achieved by diligent study and instruction. Rather, it's an intuitive knowledge—an assurance or confidence based upon observation. In other words, when I can see that one of my patients has in some small way, rallied (at least for the moment), I know I have made a difference. Whether that difference is physical, emotional, or even spiritual doesn't really matter. The fact is I have altered their life course.

GREGORY R. FROST, RRT

Years ago I had a favorite coffee mug. One was given to each attendee at a national medical trade show where my company was exhibiting—the *American Association of Operating Room Nurses* convention. This was back in the early 90's when healthcare was changing dramatically and Managed Care loomed on the horizon. No one was certain of the outcome, so the theme of the week-long meeting was one of 'preparation and adaptation'... or becoming more flexible by using the inevitable changes to your advantage.

As an illustration to support the philosophy, the coffee mugs had all been etched with a beautiful sailboat in motion along with a version of the popular quote attributed to Jimmy Dean: *"We can't change the wind—but we can adjust the sails."*

I think of making a difference in those terms; when you know you have absolutely no control of a situation, you can still make adjustments and modify your actions in the hope of harnessing the power of the problem—and ultimately change its direction.

The adjustments need not be major. Small things matter. I like the way children's rights advocate Marian Wright Edelman explained it: "We must not, in trying to think about how we can make a big difference, ignore the small daily differences we can make which, over time, add up to big differences that we often cannot foresee."

One of my RT colleagues agreed to take me under his wing as I began the process of re-entry into the field of Respiratory Care. While working for the school district and studying for my boards, I volunteered on weekends at a local hospital under his direction.

One of the first things he said has stuck with me, and I have embraced it as my own philosophy. He shared his approach to patient care by saying that his goal is to see his patients better by the end of a shift, than they were when he started. "If that happens," he says, "I've made a difference."

That is what's worth collecting. *That* is the experience I need. *That* is what I love. The difference I make is what I treasure. Every single patient visit, no matter how routine, whether in a hospital, home, or an extended care facility provides me with a chance to have an impact and make that small difference. Although intangible, it's what I seek. It's what I collect. And it is priceless.

As I carefully place the tear bottle back on the shelf, I'm suddenly struck by the reality of my own aging. It's hard to fathom that I am now in my sixties, married more than 40 years.

The children are grown and on their own. Grandchildren have arrived, and we've adopted a precious young boy in recent years.

Some things have faded while others are more crystalline than ever.

Having begun this journey of discovery and purpose, I continue to strive for three things; wisdom to recognize the central good, courage to make honorable choices, and the privilege of being granted permission to observe.

GREGORY R. FROST, RRT

PERMISSION TO OBSERVE

Made in the USA
Middletown, DE
09 January 2020